D0356553

CHINA:
THE CHURCH'S
LONG MARCH

Both of these titles are co-published with other organizations whose personnel live and work in these special areas of the world. They have expertise and information not usually available to the rest of us. The authors are dependable, experienced Christians of unquestionable integrity and commitment. While their names may be new to some of us, they have lived, worked and experienced what God is doing in those hidden places on planet earth.

Africa: A Season for Hope
Edited by W. Dayton Roberts
Co-published with World Vision International
China: The Church's Long March
by David H. Adeney
Co-published with Overseas Missionary Fellowship, Singapore

Watch for forthcoming books in this series on the *Middle East, Afghanistan* and other areas of Christian concern in the world today.

CHINA:
THE CHURCH'S LONG MARCH

BY DAVID H. ADENEY

FOREWORD BY
JAMES HUDSON TAYLOR III

CO-PUBLISHED BY

Regal Books
Division of Gospel Light
2300 Knoll Drive
Ventura, CA 93003

OMF Publishers
Overseas Missionary Fellowship
2 Cluny Road
Singapore 1025, Rep. of Singapore

Rights for publishing this book in other languages are contracted by Gospel Literature International (GLINT) foundation. GLINT also provides technical help for
the adaptation, translation, and publishing of Bible study resources and books in
scores of languages worldwide. For further information, contact GLINT, Post
Office Box 6688, Ventura, California 93006, U.S.A., or the publisher.

Published by Regal Books
A Division of GL Publications
Ventura, California 93006
Printed in U.S.A.

Library of Congress Cataloging in Publication Data

Adeney, David H. (David Howard)
    China, the church's long march.
    Bibliography: p.
    1. China—Church history—20th century. I. Title.
BR1288.A33   1985   275.1'082   85-25666
ISBN 0-8307-1096-5

Contents

APPENDICES

Foreword

China has suddenly re-emerged from self-imposed isolationism to the forefront of world attention. Vice-Premier Deng Xiaoping, octogenarian notwithstanding, is leading his nation of more than a billion people into a new and exciting era of international relations, as well as agricultural and industrial development. Under the banner of his Four Modernizations, China is being transformed economically, socially and even ideologically at a pace that is difficult to keep up with. The China kaleidoscope can be dizzying!

Even the religious policy of this Communist government boggles the mind and defies easy generalizations. Who could have foreseen—after 15 years of obscurantism and the scourge of the Cultural Revolution—that more than 2,000 official Protestant churches would be open today, not to speak of hundreds of thousands of informal house meeting points; that more than 1.5 million Bibles would be printed, and even such books as *Bible Stories* and *Pilgrim's Progress* printed by the government's Social Science Press as illustrations of the Western cultural heritage. It is reported that the initial reprinting of 200,000 copies of *Pilgrim's Progress* was sold out in three days. And now, in a complete reversal of the position taken by leading representatives of the Three-Self Patriotic Movement during their official visit to Europe in 1982, the Amity Foundation has been established, welcoming major input from abroad in financial and personnel resources. The Foundation will focus on social concern, education and publishing.

The government's move to decentralize the economy and to encourage regional initiative and even competition is also reflected in invitations from provincial, municipal and institutional authorities for Christian organizations abroad to share in China's Four Modernizations. A Norwegian mission is being asked to set up a whole new university in Guangdong Province. The national government and a municipal government join in matching the investment of a Christian entrepreneur from Singapore in a Management and Technological Consultancy Research and Training Center. Repeated requests come from former mission hospitals for medical personnel to come and lecture, and serve on the staff.

At the same time, China is still very much under a Marxist-Leninist form of government that insists on the dictatorship of the Communist Party. Theoretically, in this type of totalitarian structure, no unit of society, not even the Church, is free or on its own. All are mobilized for maximum production and modernization, just as all are also subject to surveillance and indoctrination. Independent organization of Christians in such a system is technically not allowed. That hundreds of thousands of such groups do in fact exist is due to many factors—flexibility in implementing policy, quality of Christian character reflected in personal integrity, civic responsibility and economic contribution and lack of official church organization in the countryside where 80 percent of China's population lives.

David Adeney arrived in China to begin his missionary service in 1934 on the eve of the Chinese Communist Party's epic Long March. It was also a critical period in the Chinese Church's Long March. During the three decades following the Boxer Uprising of 1900, strong Chinese leadership had been steadily emerging. With Japan's aggression against China, an enormous migration took place as millions of Chinese fled from the occupied eastern provinces into the northwest, west and southwest provinces. In the providence of God, this served to advance the gospel as thousands of displaced Christians entered areas and lived among peoples never before penetrated by the gospel. It was Acts 11:19-21 all over again.

The decade of the '40s brought a great evangelical awakening among students. Beginning in the western provinces of Yunnan, Sichuan and Shaanxi, it was spearheaded by young leaders such as Calvin Chao and Moses Yu. Now back in China at the close of World War II, David and Ruth Adeney joined these Chinese colleagues in developing the Inter-Varsity Movement. Together with Wang Mingdao, David Yang Shaotang, Marcus Cheng, Jia Yuming and many others, they built a spiritual fellowship that would be sorely tested in the Chinese Church's Long March. Yet, were they not fellow workers with One who said, "I will build my church, and the gates of Hades will not overcome it" (Matt. 16:18, *NIV*)?

Though under sustained attack, the Church in China has not just survived, it has actually flourished. From 1 million believers in 1951, when the Adeneys along with other missionaries made their reluctant exodus, the number of Christians in China today may have reached a staggering 50 million. Such growth reveals something of the dimensions of the spiritual revolution now taking place in the aftermath of the Cultural Revolution—a phenomenon that even the Communist leaders have openly described as "a crisis of faith" in Communism.

In *China: The Church's Long March*, David Adeney not only chronicles the many trials of our brothers and sisters in Christ, their triumphs and failures, but also highlights important lessons we can learn from them. Here is a moving testimony of God's faithfulness and sovereign reign in all human history and timely lessons in the true nature of the Church, the power of the Word and of prayer, the importance of lay witness, the purifying effect of suffering and the power of love in community.

David Adeney writes from a heart of love for China and for our Christian brothers and sisters there. For 50 years he has lived and breathed China. This book is a call to understanding, action and prayer. Surely we can give no greater or more meaningful response than to stand with Christians in China in prevailing prayer.

James Hudson Taylor III
Singapore

Publisher's Preface

The Stone Age Sawi tribesman standing in his dugout canoe in the steaming jungles of Irian Jaya told Don Richardson, missionary-author of *Peace Child,* that he felt sorry for people who had to live "out there on the edge," and away from his village with its abundance of leeches, mosquitoes, fungi and snakes. The Sawi's worldview is centered in his tribe, village, culture and faith. And he is a devout Christian.

The upscale business person in midtown Manhattan, or the Orange County executive living in the beguiling climate of the California coast, may smile indulgently at the Sawi's naivete. Surely the best of life and life-styles is to be found in the influential centers of the free world. We are better informed, thanks to the *Los Angeles Times, Cable News,* thought-provoking books and periodicals and travel experiences to fashionable places in the world. But there too our world-class life-styles are provincial at best. We are captive by our own cultures, values and a limited worldview.

The young parents who move to small-town America for the rural environment to escape the corrosion of urban culture and raise their children in a wholesome place feel somewhat sorry for others who aren't able to do the same. Their worldview is often limited to the county line.

Recently a missionary friend working in eastern Europe was surprised to hear from a Christian who works in the very dangerous task of Bible distribution in one of the most oppressed countries express the conviction that it is easier to be a Christian in his Communist-dominated country than in the secure West where there is no struggle and the dangers are more subtle.

Jesus commanded His disciples to broaden their viewpoints and see fields ripe and ready for the harvest. The worldview of each of those disciples was limited to say the least. It was the great apostle Paul whose magnificent obsession to carry the gospel to the Gentile world was generated from a vision on a dusty road, giving him a worldview that more closely resembled God's view of His creation.

To most Christians in the free world, the Great Commission has become a big passe. We look with some satisfaction on our sizeable missionary force and the dramatic growth of the Church of Jesus Christ in some of the distant places of the world such as Asia, Africa, the Middle East, Latin America, and even behind the Iron Curtain.

God's mighty acts today in many remote places are more exciting than the book of Acts itself. For example, the most conservative estimates are that the Church of Jesus Christ in mainland China has grown more than tenfold since the missionaries left at the end of the 1940s. Comparably, the Church in the free world of the West has had no real growth in the same period and in many places is in a decline.

The last 15 years of the twentieth century will see more than a billion people added to the earth's population bringing the total to over 6 billion, "neighbors" of ours for whom Jesus Christ died, and to whom He commanded us to go. More than half of that new billion people will be under 20 years of age and only a few are alive today. Is this to be an overwhelming obstacle or an unparalleled opportunity?

Younger people are usually more open to new ideas, and even to the gospel, than older people, more aware of their own needs and the bankruptcy of the world's system. And these young people will live in the third-world areas of Asia, Africa, Latin America and the Middle East, areas of turmoil and political instability, famine and oppression. Interestingly, these are areas of unprecedented growth of the Church of Jesus Christ. Today the mighty movement of God's Spirit over the face of the earth is bringing about the planting of His Church in record numbers.

Of the 5 billion people alive today, about 25 percent consider themselves to be Christians. Another 25 percent are within the potential reach of the witness of Christians within their own cultures. Of the roughly 27,000 people groups, or cultures on earth, 10,000 are in this 50 percentile.

Yet over 50 percent of the earth's population, consisting of some 17,000 people groups, are outside the reach of the Christian Church. They have no opportunity to hear the gospel or see it lived, no missionaries and little hope. That is, unless Christians from other cultures and languages go to them. For example, the Korean Presbyterian Church plans to send out 10,000 cross-cultural foreign missionaries by the year 2000. Remarkable as that is, it is not even one person for each of the 17,000 unreached people groups.

What will it take on your part? On our part? When Jesus commanded His disciples to raise their sights He was broadening their worldview.

Raised awareness of both God's plan and the world's need produces a reordering of priorities of time and resources. Reordered priorities produce a willingness to pray to the Lord of the harvest to send forth the laborers into His harvest.

Our worldview needs enlarging. We need to broaden our sights. Never have we Christians in the West had such an abundance of money resources, opportunities, communication technology, swift and safe travel, open doors to vast areas of the nations of the earth, medical resources to combat diseases, technology to help people become self-sustaining, and the list could go on and on. Will we hoard all these blessings of God and indulge ourselves while the world around us suffers?

Hard questions seldom have easy answers, yet the answers to these questions may determine the eternal destiny of countless millions of people and the future of the Church of Jesus Christ. Jesus said that the end would not come until the gospel had been preached to all nations or "people groups" (see Matt. 24:14).

Every single one of the 6 billion people on the earth in the year 2000 will be a person made in the image of God, whom God loves and for whom Christ died. They will be our "neighbors." Jesus said that it is up to us and that He has put all the resources of heaven at our disposal to complete the task.

To that end, Regal Worldview Books is our modest attempt to help broaden the worldview of Christians, to raise awareness, to expand prayer support and to increase allocation of resources of people and funds to finish the task.

William T. Greig, Jr., Publisher
Regal Worldview Books

Acknowledgments

This book could never have been written without the help of my colleagues in the Overseas Missionary Fellowship who have assisted in research work, supplied information, organized the notes and made valuable suggestions.

Other friends have also read the manuscript and I have much appreciated their comments. I am especially grateful to the editors and to Karen Lowes, who has spent many long hours working on the computer.

My wife Ruth has encouraged me to keep going and has been patient with the papers that have been spread all over the house! I am thankful for the materials provided by various organizations referred to in the notes and in the list of resources at the end of the book.

Above all, I would acknowledge the work of the Holy Spirit in the lives of Christians in China, whose witness has made this book possible.

INTRODUCTION:
These 50 Years

Old church buildings packed with worshipers three times every Sunday. Ardent believers gathering together in small groups secretly in their homes. Large country churches with hundreds of baptisms each. Small evangelistic teams persecuted by local authorities, with some leaders in prison. Individual Christians meeting with their families, afraid to join any church group.

God has raised up a remarkable Christian witness in the world's most populous nation. After 30 years without missionaries, and in spite of intense persecution, the Church in China is now stronger and larger than before the 1949 Revolution.[1] That kind of growth is indeed amazing. At the same time, the Chinese Church is beset by bewildering problems. Few people would want to be called "China experts," expected to explain the intricacies of the present situation.

Yet Christians in the West need to be informed about developments in the Chinese Church. We must try to understand the nature of the problems facing Christians who live in a Communist society. What was the secret of their survival and growth in the years of suffering during the Cultural Revolution? What is their attitude now to the new forms of testing that have come with the government's drive to modernize the country?

Today, various voices are coming from the Chinese Church. Some write about it, relying entirely on reports from the Three-Self Patriotic Movement (TSPM),[2] the government-recognized organization dealing with Church affairs. Others write from the point of view of the independent house-church leaders, who believe that the TSPM will only restrict the growth of the Church and that to join it would be to compromise their faith.

The purpose of this book is to listen to witnesses from the Chinese Church and to study documents relating to government and Church religious policy. In doing that, we seek to gain a balanced view of the progress of God's Kingdom in China. We who pray "Thy kingdom come" naturally long to see the name of Christ proclaimed throughout the world—not neglecting the almost one-quarter of the world's population who live in the People's Republic of China.

The first two chapters look at the historical background of Christianity in China and note some changes that have taken place since 1978. I approach this discussion from my own experience in China as a missionary prior to the 1949 Revolution and then from the perspective of seven subsequent visits to China since 1978.

The remaining chapters deal with various issues, including material and spiritual problems in the society as a whole. We will consider the government's attitude to religion and the ways in which different Chinese Christians are responding. Our discussion concludes with an examination of the characteristics of the house churches, the problems faced by the Chinese Christians in them, and the believers' relationship to the worldwide Church.

During the past 50 years, I have learned much from Chinese friends in China and throughout Southeast Asia. Those of us who have lived in China for many years think back to the great number of Chinese friends who have enriched our lives. It is impossible to express all their fellowship has meant. We deeply appreciate the Chinese culture and the resourcefulness and endurance that have enabled the people to survive the sufferings and upheavals of the past 50 years.[3]

The faithfulness of Christians in the midst of unbelievable cruelty has made us ask whether our own faith would have remained strong during such testing.

Some of our friends did fail; those who remained true were conscious of their own weaknesses. Recognizing both the failures of the past and the dangers that lie ahead, those Christians would never want the Chinese Church to be idealized. Remembering our own failure to pray, we realize above all that it is only by the sovereign grace of God and by His power that the Church in China stands firm today.

A Call to China

My own fellowship with the Church in China started 50 years ago when I arrived from England with a party of new China Inland Mission (CIM) workers.[4] I had become interested in China 10 years earlier through Stanley Houghton, a teacher at Monkton Combe school. Houghton later became headmaster of Chefoo, the CIM school for missionaries' children which our own children attended many years later.

Before he left for China, Stanley Houghton introduced me to the biography of Hudson Taylor and to other books about China. I was thrilled by A. E. Glover's *A Thousand Miles of Miracle*, the story of missionaries narrowly escaping death during the Boxer Rebellion in 1900 (see glossary). A little map of China, which showed its vast population in contrast with the number of Christians, focused my concern on the multitudes who had no opportunity to hear the gospel of Jesus Christ.

Stanley Houghton sailed for China, and a couple of years later at a camp for boys one of the leaders warned me against the danger of being a half-and-half Christian. Committing my life to the complete service of Jesus Christ, I knew already fulfilling that goal would take me to China.

Preparing for Service

I finished high school just before Christmas 1929. During the next eight months before entering Cambridge University, I joined a group of dedicated young men preparing for pioneer missionary service. They were older than I and with them I experienced the joys and sorrows of open-air evangelism and Sunday School work in the London slums. The reports I heard of mission work in many fields further strengthened my sense of call to China.

A year after entering Cambridge, I was appointed student missionary secretary for the Christian Union and later for the whole British Inter-Varsity Fellowship. We formed the Inter-Varsity Missionary Fellowship with its motto "Evangelize to a Finish." Many of our members went on to serve God on the mission fields of the world.

My own desire to serve in China was tested when the doctor who examined me reported to the China Inland Mission that I was a "poor risk." Then came the day when the CIM council met to decide whether they would accept me. In my regular Bible reading that same morning, I came upon the words, "As thy days, so shall thy strength be" (Deut. 33:25, *KJV*).

Later, when I was interviewed by a doctor on the council, I saw the same words hanging on the wall of his office. My long-term commitment and the confirmation God had already given me persuaded the council to accept me. And so, for the past 50 years, I have been a "poor risk."

Because I had been active in England working among young people, I had hoped to have a student ministry in China. However, the mission leaders asked me to serve my first seven years working with country churches, so I would understand the background from which the students came. Not until after World War II did I have the opportunity to begin a student ministry in China.

My Early Years in China

When our group of new CIM workers sailed up the Yangtze River to Shanghai in 1934, few people had heard of Mao Zedong. The Long March,[5] which made Mao the leader of the forces of revolution, had just started. And, at that time, we knew little of the reasons behind the rapid growth of the Communist Party.

Before leaving Shanghai, I had an interview with Dixon Edward Hoste, successor to Hudson Taylor as general director of the China Inland Mission. Hoste had been a member of the Cambridge Seven, the group of young men who caused such a sensation in 1885 when they gave up promising futures in England to become missionaries to China.[6] Even in old age,

Hoste's bearing was upright, his mind keen. He was a great man of prayer, and seemed to have insight into the dangers that lay ahead. Realizing my enthusiasm for the student work at home I had so recently left, he said, "Mr. Adeney, beware of national pride. It shows itself just like a man who has been eating garlic."

To the Chinese, Christianity too often seemed a "foreign religion." Some missionaries, perhaps unconsciously, were overly proud of the achievements of their home countries. They were too sure of the superiority of Western culture.

Early in my missionary experience I was confronted with the terrible realization of connections being made between missionary work and imperialism. Not many miles from the beautiful pagoda in the Yangtze River city of Huaining where our language school was situated, two CIM missionaries, John and Betty Stam, were captured by a Communist guerrilla band in 1934 and beheaded. The example of their faithfulness to Christ at the cost of their lives was a powerful challenge to our group of young workers. But we were hardly prepared for the sight of a foreign warship which, as a result of the executions, then anchored in the river outside our city. It was an example of the "gunboat diplomacy" (see glossary) that brought such humiliation to the people of China. Because of such unrequested actions, allegedly to protect missionaries in times of danger, Christian missions have been regarded by Marxist historians as tools of imperialism.[7]

During my six months in language school, I received my Chinese name, *Ai Deli* ("received the truth"), from our head teacher, Mr. Yan. After that, I traveled by river steamer to Hankow and then by train to Henan, a province with important archeological sites connected with China's ancient civilization. Henan, a poor, thickly populated province, suffered from the scourge of brigands (gangs of robbers) and from such natural disasters as floods and famine.

Henry Guiness, son of an early CIM medical pioneer and the father of contemporary British author Os Guiness, met me at the Henan railway station. As my fellow worker, he introduced me to life in the area. Henry was indefatigable. He was especially appreciated by the young people as he played his trumpet and taught them to sing both Western and Chinese hymns. On that first bicycle ride along rough and dusty roads, I thought I would never be able to keep up with him. But during the years ahead, I rode thousands of miles by bicycle myself, visiting small churches scattered among Henan's villages and market towns.

Soon after our arrival at the mission station of Hiangcheng, we climbed a nearby hill and looked out over the plain, dotted with hundreds of villages. Later, Henry and my new language teacher Mr. Wang and I would go out preaching in those villages. After a year or two, we spent a month in a country-church ministry, living with the family of the church custodian. Through that kind of close contact with the people, I gradually learned the Mandarin language. During our time in Henan, churches were planted, and we saw spiritual growth.

In the early days, with limited language, we had times of discouragement. One day, instead of joining the other missionaries for prayer, I took my Bible and went alone into the hills. As I read through the Gospel of John, my faith was restored and I was again challenged to continue my language study.

Encouragement also came through Chinese friends like David Yang Shaotang from Shanxi. After he led a series of meetings in our area, I joined him for a month as a member of his "spiritual work team." His humility in prayer, his gifted teaching of the Scriptures and the experience of going with him to preach in the villages made a lasting impression on me.

Halfway through my first term of service, my prayer for a life partner was answered. An Anglo-American alliance was formed when I met and married another CIM missionary, Ruth Temple of Morristown, Minnesota. We went to live in Fangcheng (the "square city"), where my teacher Mr. Wang was the evangelist. Our home consisted of two rooms at the end of a large building that had been adapted as a meeting place for the church.

In addition to teaching, preaching and itinerating among the many village churches, we also ministered to refugees and the victims of bombing raids. I came to appreciate Ezekiel's imagery of the watchman (see Ezek. 3:17) when Mr. Wang and I stayed in a small town that was about to be attacked by brigands. We would hear the hourly gong of the night watchman as he patrolled the dark, quiet streets.

Usually everything was peaceful, but on that occasion we were aroused by an urgent beating of the gong announcing the approach of the brigand army. With the other men of the town I went to the wall and saw nearby villages in flames. But the brigands chose not to attack a walled town that was already alerted to their presence. The next day, government soldiers arrived and the robbers disappeared.

Our church was not far from the main motor road. Once after the Yellow River, also known as "China's sorrow," had broken its banks and had flooded vast areas, thousands of refugees traveled on this road to new land allocated to them by the government. We set up a "tea station" by the side of the road, and on several occasions large groups of refugees stayed overnight with us. When one Christian group left, I accompanied them to the motor road where they went on their way singing:

> Yesterday, today, forever,
> Jesus never changes.
> All may change, but Jesus never—
> Glory to His name.
> Parents and brothers,
> All may leave me;
> Heaven and earth may pass away,
> But Jesus never changes,
> Glory to His name.[8]

Later we heard that the first thing those people did when they reached their new home was to build a little chapel and appoint one of their members pastor.

War and Witness

Not long after the floods, came war. The Long March of the Red Army ended with the setting up of a Communist stronghold in Yanan. Generalissimo Chiang Kai-shek went to Xi'an to organize further campaigns against the Communists, but was captured by one of his dissatisfied generals. The secret agreement that preceded his release committed the Nationalist armies to join the Communists in a common fight against the Japanese invaders. That agreement was soon followed by a full-scale Japanese invasion.

When Ruth and I were in Hankow for our wedding in 1938, Japanese bombers were attacking the nearby city of Wuhan. A year or two later we began to feel the effects of the war in Henan. We dug an air raid shelter in our garden and rushed there with our baby girl, Rosemary, and Chinese fellow workers when low-flying Japanese planes made bombing raids over the city.

Because the only military hospital had moved, we were asked to go out and help the wounded. A mission doctor gave us a small supply of antiseptics and first-aid instructions. I remember making daily visits to an old beggar with a terrible festering wound on his leg. The smell and presence of maggots were so bad that no one else would go near him. Because of our willingness to give even our unskilled aid, doors opened for the gospel.

On one occasion as local officials were visiting us, Japanese planes suddenly arrived, and we all took refuge under the dining room table. We had painted a red cross on the roof of our church building and were thankful that no bombs actually fell on our property, although a small bomb did hit the house next door.

The most serious danger came when a guerrilla army made up of Japanese and Koreans marched down the motor road and briefly occupied our town. Although the Christians had asked us to put up a notice saying that the church was British property, the only way to keep the invading soldiers out was for me to stand at the church door. A terrible time for any townspeople who had not fled to the hills, it was a night of horror: rape, pillage, slaughter. The next day before leaving, the Japanese officers brought us a gift of cigarettes and asked us to sign a statement that we had been well treated. They then set fire to nearby houses. As soon as they left, we went out to fight the flames.

Once again our obvious willingness to help opened people's hearts to the gospel. Two senior high school students who had been in hiding during the attack came and told me how impressed they were by the courage of a Christian friend during that time of danger. They did not want to believe in superstition, they said—such as Jesus rising from the dead— but they were willing to study the Scriptures with me. Not long afterward they too were praying to the risen Saviour. Later I met one of them while waiting for a ferry. He was on his way with other refugees to a university in the west and he told me of the difference in his life now that he was a Christian.

When the time came for our family to leave Fangcheng, we knew that the Lord had indeed established His Church in that area. We did not know about the ordeal that lay ahead—these Christians suffered terribly during the Cultural Revolution—but many years later, in 1979, we began to hear of great numbers of believers in the whole district. Fangcheng itself was called a "Jesus nest" by the Communists. Not only had the Church survived, it had grown and was sending out missionaries to other parts of China.

By the summer of 1941, our furlough was due and we were asked to travel to Shanghai. It was not an easy journey, but we were given hospitality along the way by country Christians. Ruth and Rosemary traveled on hand-drawn carts, piled high with our boxes and bedding. For days we traveled through dangerous guerrilla-controlled territory. When we reached the Japanese lines, the soldiers were so intrigued by seeing a baby they forgot to inspect our luggage.

From Shanghai we traveled with the CIM general director, Bishop and Mrs. Frank Houghton, on the *Tatsuma Maru,* the last Japanese passenger ship allowed to dock at San Francisco before Pearl Harbor. Before landing we sailed in circles for several days while a decision was made about whether the ship should discharge its passengers and cargo or return to Japan. Japanese bank accounts had been frozen and no Japanese imports were to be allowed entrance.

Thus, in the purpose of God we were able to reach the United States just before the December 1941 bombing of Pearl Harbor and to spend two years working with the newly-formed American Inter-Varsity Christian Fellowship (IVCF-USA). That turned out to be excellent preparation for ministry with Chinese students during our second term of service in China. In the meantime, our next assignment was to work on the home staff of the CIM in London.

Student Work in China

After the war, in January 1946, I was loaned by the CIM to the China Inter-Varsity Christian Fellowship under the leadership of Calvin Chao. A cable from China arrived asking me to go to Chongqing. Because the call to student work was urgent, I flew from London to India on a "flying boat," a large seaplane, leaving my family to come later by ship. That journey took three days, with stops on a river or lake each night. From India a flight over the "hump" of the Himalayas brought me to Chongqing in West China, just in time to participate in a large student winter conference. At that conference, I slept on a gymnasium floor with hundreds of university students.

Just recently, I received a letter from a Chinese who now resides in the U.S. "Don't regard me as a stranger," he wrote. "My bed was next to yours on the floor of that gym." He and innumerable others had fled from institutions in the eastern provinces to the safety of Sichuan.

During the next few years I traveled widely all over China and found the Holy Spirit at work in universities in many parts of the land. After my family arrived, we made our home in Nanjing. Shortly before the success of the Revolution in 1949, we moved into Shanghai and were there when the Communist armies entered.

For 15 months we shared the problems Christian students faced at the beginning of that new regime. In our Bible study groups we studied the principles of Scripture that would help in the new society being formed. At fellowship meetings we listened to Christians tell of the testings that came in indoctrination meetings and in self-criticism groups, when they were called on to attack other Christians.

After the Revolution

By August 1950, however, it was clear that our continued

presence could be only an embarrassment to Chinese Christians. When we said good-bye to our student friends at the Shanghai railway station, we realized great trials lay ahead of them.

After another five years with IVCF-USA, we relocated in Hong Kong. From 1956 to 1968 I was associate general secretary for the Far East with the International Fellowship of Evangelical Students (IFES), visiting university student groups from Korea to India. My successor was Chua Wee Hian, the present general secretary of IFES.

Ruth and I then moved to Singapore with the Overseas Missionary Fellowship (OMF), the new name for the CIM, to start the Discipleship Training Center (DTC). The DTC was a cross-cultural community for university graduates from various countries, many of whom I had met in student work during previous years.

During those years, we received little news of Christian students in China. Only after the death of Mao in 1976 did doors begin to open and communication with friends in China become possible once again.

Our Knowledge of China Today

Our present knowledge of what has been happening in China comes from four sources. In addition to official information from the TSPM, there are:

1. Reports from Chinese Christians who have come out to Hong Kong or to Western countries. Some of these men and women have been active in independent house-church meetings. Others have been associated with TSPM-related churches.

2. Stories from Christian Chinese travelers, living in other countries, who have visited friends and relatives in China. Many of them have had access to country villages.

3. Letters, documents and tapes written or recorded inside China.

4. Reports from Western Christians who know the language and have been able to contact friends in China.

Before focusing more specifically on the developments of the past 35 years, we must be sure to have a right attitude, starting with a spirit of thanksgiving. We rejoice that together with the Church in China we are part of the worldwide Body of Christ. Just as nothing can separate us from the love of Christ, so also nothing can separate us from the unity that is in Christ. Physical distance and political barriers may hinder us from experiencing full fellowship, but by faith we stand together as fellow sinners who have been reconciled by the "blood of his cross" (Col. 1:20, *KJV*). We have nothing to boast of in ourselves, but together we glory in having "been made partakers of the inheritance of the saints in light . . . delivered . . . from the power of darkness and translated . . . into the kingdom of his dear Son" (Col. 1:12,13, *KJV*).

We do not regard Chinese Christians as a younger Church or as a distant mission field. Rather they are fellow pilgrims and workers in the task of proclaiming the gospel which Paul says is to be "preached to every creature which is under heaven" (Col. 1:23).

This book is written with the prayer that Christians in other parts of the world may learn from the experience of the Church in China. We trust that their example of faithfulness in the midst of great suffering will cause us to dedicate ourselves in a new way to stand with them in their spiritual battles. We seek to understand their present situation and the nature of the trials they still face, in order to pray more intelligently for them.

CHINA REVISITED
A Link with the Past

While speaking at a student conference in Hong Kong, I learned of an opportunity to join a small tour group visiting mainland China. So in August 1978, with two Christian friends, I returned to China after an absence of 28 years.

Our visit was the culmination of years of praying and waiting for news of the Church and of my former fellow Chinese workers. Often during the 12 years when my family and I were living in Hong Kong, and I was working with students throughout Asia, I went to the high point near the Hong Kong/China border. From there I gazed across the duck farms and high barbed wire fences to the other side of the river. Those towns were so near, yet they were almost completely cut off from the outside world.

We had little news of what was going on in the Chinese Church. But by the mid-'70s, reports were coming to us increasingly of the work of the Holy Spirit in house churches scattered in most of the provinces of China.

The New China

Entering China on that first return visit in 1978 was very different from the way in which most tourists enter there today. Instead of speeding across the border in air-conditioned trains, our tour group had to change trains and carry our baggage across the bridge that separates the two territories. Leaving the

Hong Kong police and British soldiers at one end of the bridge, we passed the green-uniformed People's Liberation Army soldiers and entered the Chinese immigration and customs offices. The border town of Shenzhen, then little more than a fishing village, now has become a modern city with high-rise office buildings and factories—a symbol of the tremendous economic growth that has taken place in China during the past few years.

On that first visit, no churches were open except for one Protestant and one Roman Catholic church, both mainly for foreigners, in Beijing (Peking). It was very difficult to make contact with Christians. Great changes were already taking place, however. Two years before in Hong Kong, I had watched a television program showing the funeral of Mao Zedong. Later I saw the rejoicing that followed the arrest of the Gang of Four (see glossary), the ultra-leftist associates of Mao that included his wife and who shared responsibility for the Cultural Revolution.

In April 1978, Chairman Hua Guofeng,[1] Mao's successor, was attacked in a poster in Beijing which asked questions about the Tian An Men riots.[2] The poster expressed support for the late Premier Zhou Enlai's more moderate policies as well as dissatisfaction with the Cultural Revolution.

Deng Xiaoping—China's present de facto ruler and political strategist—was then urging the Communist Party to "seek truth from facts." Already discussions were going on concerning Mao's responsibility for the disaster of the Cultural Revolution. On July 1, the fifty-seventh anniversary of the founding of the Chinese Communist Party (CCP), newspapers all over the country printed a speech that Mao had made in 1962 in which he confessed that he had made errors during the "Great Leap Forward."[3] The Party was now acknowledging that Mao was fallible. The real struggle between Hua and Deng surfaced late in 1978 in a poster campaign at Democracy Wall, a public place in Beijing used to display posters criticizing government policies.

Thus, at the time of my first return visit, not only was the Gang of Four being blamed for the ravages of the Cultural Revolution, but there were questions concerning Mao Zedong himself.

About this time the government announced that several

thousand Chinese students would be sent to study abroad. That development immediately awakened hope in the minds of young people, many of whom started to learn English. The police were told not to interfere when they saw young people starting conversations with foreign tourists.

In Beijing alone, during a four-month period, more than a million books for the study of English were sold. The ban on listening to foreign radio stations was lifted, and the Far East Broadcasting Company (FEBC), whose station is known as "the Voice of Friendship," began to receive hundreds of letters. By mid-1984, the number had grown to 45,000.[4]

We were impressed by the friendliness of the people when we slipped away from the tour and went for a walk in the crowded streets of the city. A couple of young carpenters invited us into their home and gave us tea. Later, when we were looking for some of the closed church buildings, an engineering student and an older man brought out a table and chair and invited us to sit and talk with them. People were eager to hear what was happening outside China.

Finding Christians

Whenever we asked about Christians we were told that just a few of the older people believed. The Bible itself was still an illegal book. For example, a notice sent to a certain Chinese Christian by the customs office stated: "Any literature detrimental to the economic, social and political good of society cannot be received." Scripture portions enclosed in a letter addressed to him were not delivered, and he was asked to inform his overseas friend not to send any such literature in the future.

On one occasion, while waiting for a friend on a busy street, we were surrounded by a group of young people who had many questions. All of them had been brought up in a Marxist society with no opportunity to study matters of faith. As we talked, I told them that although I recognized the importance of material things, I was convinced that all of us have spiritual needs which can be satisfied only through faith in God.

One young man spoke up and agreed that faith was useful.

"But only a few old people," he added, "believe in religion." He insisted, however, that young people would be free to believe if they wanted to.

As the crowd broke up and began to walk away, another young man joined me. He started by saying, "What the man in the crowd has just said is untrue. There is no freedom to believe." He then began to pour out his deep feelings of dissatisfaction.

I discovered that, although he was not a Christian, he had a hunger for spiritual things and came from a Christian home. His family had suffered greatly during the Cultural Revolution. Their home had been ransacked and all their books, including the Bible, had been taken away. We were able to get away from the crowd and once we reached a quiet place, I gave him a New Testament. We agreed to meet again.

The next day I met the young man's elderly father who was hospitalized. He confided, "I am a Christian, but I cannot tell anyone." We also met other members of this family in their very primitive little house where they had been sent when their home was taken away during the Cultural Revolution. Knowing how much they had suffered, I rejoiced to be able to tell them of God's love and faithfulness and to pray with them.

At the time of that first visit, Christians were thankful for the changes that had come following the fall of the Gang of Four, but they were still uncertain about the future. They were also very cautious about revealing their meeting places unless they were sure they could trust the person to whom they were speaking.

One member of our tour met a Christian woman in the park. She would not speak about the house church she attended, but told the story of her husband's conversion. As a CCP member he had strongly opposed her Christian faith, but during a serious illness his attitude had completely changed. While his wife was praying earnestly for him, he passed through a near-death experience, seeing his own body lying on the bed and listening to a beautiful song. That convinced him that there was something more to life than just our physical bodies. At that moment he began to improve, and after his recovery his wife was able to lead him to faith in Christ.

Already in 1978, Christians were being released from prison. Following Deng's resumption of power and the more relaxed domestic climate, Christians were able to meet more freely for worship. One friend wrote of the joy of being able to sing hymns in their home again without fear that neighbors would report them to the police—called the Public Security Bureau. Government officials stated that churches would be opened, and plans were being made to reestablish the TSPM, which had controlled Protestant church activities before the Cultural Revolution. But long before any churches were opened, thousands of Christians, some in large groups, were already meeting in homes scattered throughout the country.

Nonetheless, in spite of that indigenous growth in house churches and the rapid increase in the number of Christians in some areas, it was obvious that Christianity was still regarded by many as a foreign religion linked to imperialism. I saw evidence of that in a museum we visited early on in our tour. While the guide was giving a talk in English to the others, I walked around the exhibits and, to my surprise, discovered a picture of a mission hospital. Its Chinese caption stated: "Missionaries came not because they loved the people and wanted to heal the sick, but in order to manipulate the people and further their own political aims." Years later I was to meet a Chinese scholar in Norway who mentioned that many people had been told that Christian doctors came to China mainly to perform experiments on their patients.

Chinese Church History: A Brief Summary

Ever since the Revolution, the Communists have emphasized the fact that missionaries are agents of imperialism. It has often been stated that the early Christian missionaries entered China at the point of the bayonet. To understand those charges we must look back at the history of Christianity in China. Nor can the experience of the Chinese Church during the last 35 years be divorced from the attempts by Christians to evangelize that country. The ebb and flow of Chinese Church history of the past 1,350 years helps us understand not only recent changes, but also those likely to take place.

Nestorian and Catholic Missionaries

The first missionaries, Nestorian Christians, reached China in A.D. 635 (Tang dynasty). Franciscan monks arrived in the thirteenth and fourteenth centuries (Yuan dynasty), and Jesuit missionaries in the sixteenth and seventeenth centuries (Ming dynasty). All of those early missionary attempts failed to take root in Chinese culture, and Christianity continued to be seen as a foreign religion.

While visiting Christian students at Northwest University in Xi'an in 1947, I saw the Nestorian tablet erected in A.D. 781, which commemorated the coming of the first Nestorian monk, Alopen. These Nestorian missionaries came from countries east of the Roman empire; their doctrines varied slightly from those of Constantinople and Rome. Most of the dozens of names on that tablet are not Chinese.

Nestorian missionaries traveled with merchants along the "silk road" from Persia across central Asia. Their converts seemed to have come largely from Mongolian people and from foreigners living in China. Many of those Christians fled or were killed during the severe persecution of all religious institutions in 845. Over 400 years later, in 1288, Marco Polo found traces of the Nestorians; there had been a revival of their work under the Mongol Yuan dynasty which conquered China in 1211.

Kublai Khan, one of the great rulers of the Yuan dynasty, asked the Pope in Rome for a hundred men of learning and devotion to Christ. But it was not until 20 years later that John of Montecovino arrived at the court of Timur, Kublai Khan's successor. In those days a journey from Rome to Beijing might well take as long as three years, and many who began it would not finish. John of Montecovino baptized 6,000 and built churches. But when the Mongol dynasty fell, the Han Chinese under the Ming dynasty expelled both Nestorians and Franciscans. The Christians who remained faced persecution from those who regarded Christianity as the "religion of foreign barbarians."

Jesuit Ascendancy

China returned to deliberate isolationism from the West until the sixteenth century, when Portuguese merchants were permitted to establish a trading station in Macao, not far from Hong Kong. No foreigners were allowed to live in China at that time. Francis Xavier, the famous Jesuit missionary, died on an island near Guangzhou (Canton) in 1552. The Portuguese navy had already captured Goa (India) and Malacca (Malaya) during that era of colonial expansionism. Missionaries sailed with Spanish and Portuguese merchants to set up missions in Asian countries, and finally a foothold was gained in China.

"Rock, rock, O when wilt thou open, Rock?" Those were the words of Alessandro Valignano, vicar general to all Jesuit missions in the Far East. He realized that Christianity could never be forced on the Chinese people. Valignano brought a young Italian seminary teacher, Matteo Ricci, to Macao and in 1583 Ricci obtained permission to reside in Guangzhou. While there he adopted Chinese dress and expressed his admiration for China's ancient civilization. He also took advantage of the scientific achievements of the West and introduced some of the recent developments in astronomy and mathematics, hoping to win the respect of scholars and introduce them to the Christian faith as well.

Ricci sought to restate the Christian gospel in Confucian thought and terminology, while at the same time opposing Buddhist and Daoist (Taoist) concepts. He emphasized the importance of loyalty and respect to the emperor and ancestors. After he finally established residence in Beijing, some scholars and officials were converted. He won the approval of the imperial court through his skill in repairing clocks and in making maps and reliable calendars. Those who followed Ricci continued his eclectic tradition. Under the Manchu Qing dynasty, Jesuit influence continued to increase, and Emperor Kang Xi employed missionaries as personal advisors. He even published an edict declaring the legality of the Christian faith.

By that time, however, a serious dispute—known as the rites controversy—had risen between the Jesuits and Dominicans. The Dominicans accused the Jesuits of compromising in their attempt to present the faith in a way that would be acceptable in Confucian culture. They especially objected to allowing converts to participate in ancestor worship, a practice the Jesuits claimed was a form of reverence, a civil rite, and not religious worship. The Jesuit use of the Chinese words *Shangdi* "the heavenly ruler" and *Tian* "heaven" in referring to God was also criticized because of their connection with Chinese concepts of deity. The rites controversy finally resulted in papal intervention. When the Pope ruled against the Jesuits' occasionally syncretistic attempts to contextualize Christianity, the emperor felt that his authority was being challenged by a foreign ruler. He expelled the papal legate and ordered all missionaries who did not follow Ricci's policy to leave the country.

Emperor Kang Xi's successor, Qian Long, issued edicts against Christianity and ushered in another period of persecution. Once again the followers of Christ were attacked because of their connection with a foreign power. (Similar problems have reappeared in recent years, resulting in a rift between the Chinese Catholic Patriotic Association and the Vatican.) At the close of the sixteenth century, Catholic Christians survived in scattered underground groups. Catholic priests could operate only in secrecy, often at the risk of their lives.

The failure of the Jesuit mission was due partly to the dominant role of the priests and to the emphasis on institutions, which were usually controlled by the missionaries. Catholic Christians tended to live in separate communities.

The Protestant Mission Era

The opening decades of Protestant missions in China coincided with the rapid rise of colonialism and the extension of militant Western imperialism in Africa and Asia.

In 1807, Robert Morrison, a Scottish Presbyterian, reached Guangzhou, the only city open to foreign merchants. He traveled on an American ship because no British ship would take him. Merchants of the East India Company (EIC) feared that the presence of missionaries might jeopardize their opportunities for trade.

On the way out, the ship's captain reportedly asked, "Mr. Morrison, do you expect that you can make any impact on that great nation?"

"No," Morrison said, "but I expect that *God* will."

Morrison's first months were difficult, but he made such rapid progress in language study that before long the East India Company was glad to appoint him as a translator. That position gave him the status he needed to stay on in China as an employee of the EIC.

Only a very few Chinese became Christians during Morrison's stay in China, but the inscription on his tombstone pays tribute to the importance of his work in translating the Scriptures there. On a number of occasions I have stood by his grave, hidden in a quiet corner of a cemetery in Macao, not far from the ruins of the Roman Catholic cathedral that later inspired the writing of the well-known hymn, "In the Cross of Christ I glory, towering o'er the wrecks of time." For both Morrison and his colleague, William Milne, it was a difficult and lonely life; both of their wives died.

Finally, other missionaries began to arrive, although in the early days their work was confined to the areas of Guangzhou and Macao. Still other missionaries waited in Singapore and busied themselves in preparing Chinese literature. Karl Gutzlaff of the Netherlands Missionary Society traveled up and down the coast on merchant ships that sometimes carried opium. Whenever possible, he distributed Christian literature in the ports they visited—without realizing that his identification with opium-carrying ships also identified Christianity with opium.

Not until after the first Opium War and the signing of the Nanjing Treaty in 1842 did the door open for merchants and missionaries to reside and travel in China. Hong Kong, then little more than a barren island, was ceded to Britain, and five treaty ports were opened.

Following the second Opium War, the 1858 Treaty of Tianjin opened additional ports for trade and permitted foreigners to travel throughout the empire. Religious toleration clauses stated that foreigners and Chinese converts who "peaceably teach and practice the principles of Christianity, shall in no case be interfered with or molested." The *extra territoriality rights* granted to the British were also given to citizens of the United States and France in similar treaties. Such rights meant that missionaries now could live in the treaty ports under the legal protection of their own country's laws.

China had banned the use of opium, but in the "unequal treaties" instituted after the Opium Wars, the British also forced China to legalize the iniquitous opium trade. Thus the opening of the doors for merchants and missionaries was inevitably linked with opium. What a travesty it was that after the Chinese rulers had realized the evil of opium addiction and sought to prevent the entry of that drug into China, the British authorities, furthering their own commercial interests, supported its continuance.

Even though Christians in England protested against the opium trade, and a vote of censure failed in Parliament by only nine votes, missionaries inevitably found themselves associated with the colonial powers. In spite of the unfavorable atmosphere created by the "unequal treaties" just mentioned, with the resulting prejudice against foreigners, missionaries could not withdraw from responsibility to take the good news of the Kingdom of God to the unreached population in China. Just as Paul used his Roman citizenship to facilitate his missionary journeys, so the early pioneers—even when deeply disturbed by the policies of their own governments—took advantage of the doors opened to them. The situation was further complicated by the decline of the Qing dynasty and the subsequent widespread social unrest and fighting between various factions. Nevertheless, we recognize the sovereign power of God over even the evils of imperialism in opening the door for the sacrificial service of the early pioneer missionaries.

The first missionaries lived in business settlements, where their foreign dress and life-style emphasized the foreignness of the religion they preached. A few started to visit nearby towns. When Hudson Taylor arrived in 1854 he was eager to get away from the foreign enclaves and to preach in the countryside. Many of his compatriots strongly criticized him for discarding foreign dress, but he was encouraged by the changed attitude of the people when he appeared in Chinese clothes. He wrote:

> I am fully satisfied that the native dress is an absolute prerequisite . . . quietly settling among the people, obtaining free, familiar, and unrestrained communication with them, conciliating their prejudices, attracting their esteem and confidence, and so living as to be examples to them of what Chinese Christians should be, require the adoption not merely of this costume but also of their habits to a very considerable extent . . . . There is perhaps no country in the world in which religious toleration is carried to so great an extent as in China; the only objection that prince or people have to Christianity is that it is a foreign religion and that its tendencies are to approximate believers to foreign nations . . . The foreign appearance of the chapels and indeed the foreign air given to everything connected with religion have very largely hindered the rapid dissemination of the truth among the Chinese. But why need such a foreign aspect be given to Christianity? The Word of God does not require it; nor I conceive would reason justify it. It is not their denationalization but their Christianization that we seek.[5]

Before founding the China Inland Mission in 1865, Hudson Taylor had experienced the precariousness of life in China. Without modern medical knowledge, the average life of a pioneer missionary was seven years. Further, the early pioneers constantly faced danger from lawlessness in the countryside.

The mid-nineteenth century was marked by dynastic decline and by the ravages caused by rival armies. From 1851 to 1864 the country suffered terribly from the Taiping Rebellion, led by an unsuccessful candidate for the civil service examination. Hong Xiuquan (Hung Hsiu-ch'uan) had been influenced by Christian tracts and in a dream from *Shangdi* felt that he was called to rid China of idolatry and corruption. He set out to overthrow the Manchu dynasty and replace it with a heavenly kingdom named

Taiping (meaning "great peace").

Because Hong Xiuquan gained the support of many country people, his rebellion has been hailed as the forerunner of the Communist Revolution. But in these contemporary tributes, no reference is made to the Christian teaching that influenced the rebellion in its early days. How different China's history might have been if that movement had continued to be directed by Christian principles. Not surprisingly, as it grew in power, Chinese of many different beliefs joined it. Mystical and superstitious elements were added, and in time the movement lost its Christian emphasis.

Hong Xiuquan became obsessed with the idea that he was the younger brother of Jesus Christ. He established his capital in Nanjing and for 10 years his armies extended their control over large areas of the country. When Shanghai was threatened, however, the foreign powers organized an army and assisted the corrupt imperial Manchu forces to destroy the Taipings. Some 20 million people were killed during the more than 10 years of that war.

By then the Manchu government was too weak to resist the growing Western encroachment. The unequal Beijing Treaty (1861) allowed missionaries to own land in China's interior, and thus led to the building up of large institutions. The Roman Catholic Church became a great landowner, and later those large institutions attracted strong criticism from Communist leaders. More and more missionaries arrived to work in schools, colleges and hospitals. They introduced Western science and technology. They were pioneers in modern methods of education, medicine and social services. They spearheaded campaigns against opium smoking, prostitution and the long-time custom of footbinding baby girls. Nonetheless, in spite of the great value of the educational system introduced by missionaries, it must be recognized that missionary institutions did *not* always produce strong spiritual Chinese leaders and self-supporting churches.

During those years, many Chinese intellectuals became antiforeign and often anti-Christian as well. At the end of the nineteenth century, China was humiliated by defeat at the hands of Japan, which resulted in the loss of Taiwan and the recognition of

Korea's independence. China was being carved up as Western nations gained spheres of influence.

Although most missionaries were not involved in political developments, some assisted their governments in drawing up treaties and legal documents. The "toleration clauses" in the unequal treaties even enabled Chinese converts to receive legal help from missionaries in cases of alleged persecution; thus they too were removed from the jurisdiction of local officials. Those unequal treaties remained in force until 1943.

Although some of China's officials recognized that China needed Western science, at the same time they stirred up the people to drive out the foreigners. An attempt by young reformers to bring change in the government culminated in the "Hundred Days" of 1898, but was defeated by the Empress Dowager Zi Xi. She supported the Boxer Uprising of 1900 which resulted in the death of more than 1,900 Protestant Chinese Christians and 30,000 Roman Catholics. In addition, 188 Protestant missionaries and children and 47 Roman Catholic priests and nuns were killed during that rebellion.

The tragedy of the Boxer Rebellion resulted in further humiliation for China. An allied army from eight nations drove out the Boxer rebels from Beijing and forced the government to make more concessions to the foreign powers and pay huge indemnities. The China Inland Mission, whose missionaries had been widely scattered, lost many workers and much property, but refused to accept payment for damages.

The nineteenth century witnessed a great increase in the number of Christians. In 1900 there were almost 113,000 Protestant Christians with 1,600 Chinese Christian workers and 2,000 missionaries. During the early years of the twentieth century, that advance continued. CIM missionaries found that the witness of faithful Chinese Christians in the midst of persecution, and the attitude of the mission in not asking for indemnity, opened people's hearts to the gospel.

The CIM became the largest mission in China, emphasizing taking the message of salvation to unreached areas. Churches were established not only among the majority Han people but also among the ethnic minorities that comprise about 5 percent of the population: tribal peoples living in the mountains of southwest China and Muslims in the far northwest. During the first decade of the twentieth century, the Shandong revival brought an evangelical awakening to North China that influenced other parts of the country as well.

Nationalism and Communism

The early twentieth century was also a time of great political change. A spirit of nationalism was growing among China's intellectuals. Seeing that reform of the old regime was impossible, they turned to revolution. Under the leadership of Sun Zhongshan (Sun Yat Sen), the Manchu dynasty was toppled in 1911 and a republic was formed. Sun Zhongshan, a Christian, had his power base in the south and was unable to form a strong central government for the whole country. Vast areas were still controlled by warlords, and for almost 40 years China suffered internal struggles and foreign invasions.

World War I not only revealed the spiritual bankruptcy of the Western nations, but it also caused China's young nationalists to give up any hope of receiving Western support in their struggle for independence. China expected that the 1919 Treaty of Versailles would restore areas formerly controlled by Germany, but instead they were given to Japan. After the Bolshevik Revolution in Russia, some Chinese intellectuals, disillusioned with the West, began to look to the Soviet Union.

The Chinese Communist Party, formed in 1921, at first cooperated with the Nationalists. Even Chiang Kai-shek, military leader in the new republic, visited Russia and for a time worked with the Communists. His successful northern expedition in 1927 brought much of the country under Nationalist control. About that time also, he broke with the Communists and killed many of their leaders, thereby starting a campaign to destroy Communist forces.

Before the conflict between the Nationalists and the Communists surfaced openly, however, a strong anti-foreign and anti-Christian movement had emerged. The "May the Fourth Movement," which began as a student protest in Beijing against the Treaty of Versailles, stirred the flames of nationalism. Students protested against Christian schools, and during the decade of the '20s anti-foreign riots occurred in many parts of the country. Large numbers of missionaries had to leave the interior and return to the coastal cities. Many left China for good. But by 1930 most missionaries had resumed their work in the interior and others were coming.

The Rise of Mao

One of the leaders of the May the Fourth Movement, Chen Duxiu, became the first chairman of the Chinese Communist Party. Mao Zedong, who had been a library assistant in Beijing University, was also present at the birth of the Party in 1921. He had read the *Communist Manifesto* and accepted the Marxist position, but unlike the Russian leaders he believed that the key to revolution lay with the peasants. After studying the situation in the rural areas of his own province, he wrote his "Report on the Investigation of the Peasants in Hunan." In it he prophesied that "several hundred million peasants will rise like a mighty storm . . . they will sweep out the imperialists, warlords, corrupt officials, local tyrants, and evil gentry into their graves."

Mao's leadership was recognized during the Long March, an action resulting from the encircling tactics of the stronger Nationalist armies in south and central China. Mao's guerrilla-war strategy and his policy of identifying with the peasants enabled 10,000 men and women to survive the 370-day, 6,000-mile retreat. Despite constant fighting and difficult terrain, the Red Army eventually reached Yanan, which then became a base for the Communist armies in northwest China.

During the chaotic years of the war with Japan, which began in 1937, Communist forces continued to enlarge their sphere of influence. Much territory came under their control during the war. After peace with Japan in 1945, the people were exhausted by the long years of war; the economy was in shambles. I remember taking a sack to the bank to pick up funds since one American dollar was worth more than a half-million local dollars.

When American attempts to bring the Nationalists and the

Communists together failed, full-scale civil war broke out. People were longing for change, and the picture Mao painted of a new society was attractive. After the defeat of the Nationalist armies, most people responded with great enthusiasm. Young people marched behind banners inscribed with words like "Go where the Revolution needs you most." Teams of students went into the countryside to work with the peasants. Everyone was called to spend long hours in political studies—since Marxists believed that only right ideology could lead to right action.

Mao's vision was to create not only a new society but a new kind of person. Millions were killed, and many others fled with the Nationalists to Taiwan. Mao thought that when he got rid of the landlord class and when the peasants acquired control of the land, he would be able to provide the ideological education that would produce a new breed of people: They would be loyal to Party leadership and would unselfishly serve their fellowmen and women. For him the young people were the hope of the future.

The climax in the working out of his plan came during the Cultural Revolution when he mobilized the Red Guards and encouraged them to destroy the remnants of the old society and all who opposed "Mao Thought." Between August and September 1966, more than 11 million young people assembled in the Tian An Men Square to hear Mao say, "Revolution is not wrong: it is right to rebel." Young people went forth with the little red book entitled *The Thoughts of Mao Zedong.* Their task was to denounce all who had any contacts with the West and to destroy the old culture and old ways of thinking. The thoughts of Mao Zedong were to triumph over every other ideology.

But Mao's dreams were never fulfilled. Drunken with power, the young Red Guards fought among themselves. When they eventually went completely out of control, turning the country into chaos, Mao had to call in the military to restore order.

The Red Guards were sent to the countryside where they became bitter and disillusioned. Their education had been disrupted, and China lost a whole generation of trained workers. Mao's death in 1976 and the subsequent arrest of the Gang of Four led to a strategic change in Communist policies.

China has now embarked on a different program to modernize the nation (see chapter 3). The people hope that the violent and painful changes of the past will be followed by a period of stability in which all will continue to search for ways to build a strong China.

Christians, who have suffered along with non-Christians, are convinced that, when the revolutionary struggle is over, the new society cannot be built on the principles of atheism. Rather it requires the love of God and the power of Christ's indwelling, which alone can create new persons and a righteous society.

MEETING OLD FRIENDS

The changes that were beginning to take shape after the death of Mao were quite evident in 1979 on my second visit to China. This time I went as leader of a small tour group. Chinese Christians could now communicate with friends outside. Worship services were being held in buildings restored by the government through the TSPM. It was also possible for visitors like myself to meet with former friends.

I will never forget my first letter from China, which I received shortly before that tour. I knew at once that it was from a friend whom I had met 25 years earlier when he was studying for his Ph.D. in America. A recent convert at that time, he was looking for Christian fellowship, and I was able to introduce him to an Inter-Varsity Bible study group. After that, he came to many IVCF conferences and was active in his witness to other students.

Just before leaving America he wrote saying that he must return to his family in China, adding, "It does not matter whether I live six months or six years, as long as I 'accomplish my course and the ministry which I received from the Lord Jesus, to testify to the gospel of the grace of God'" (Acts 20:24). I received one more letter from him, asking us not to send any books, and then there was no further word until the summer of 1979. His letter started with the words, "These 22 years my Lord has protected me," followed by a number of Scripture texts which he had found helpful during the years of great trial.

What a joy it was to hear him call my name—*David*—when I arrived in the airport in China a little later. He came with me to my hotel and told me the story of those difficult days during the Cultural Revolution.

Hard Labor and Prison

While my friend was under attack, no one would speak to him. He was not allowed to take part in any scientific research and had to spend his days digging ditches. Although deprived of his Bible, he would go out in the morning remembering the Lord's promise, "My grace is sufficient for you" (2 Cor. 12:9). In his heart he would answer, "Lord, your grace is indeed sufficient." He explained how God had led him to return to China, although he could easily have remained in America with a high academic position.

Now, because of his outstanding scientific work and his obvious love for his country, he has many opportunities to talk with young people at the close of church services. They respect him as a scientist and ask how it is that he can believe in God. In answer, he refers to the "big bang theory" of the creation of the universe, telling the students that the energy that brought the universe into being is the power of God—and the greatest power in the universe is the love of God.

In those discussions, he describes how the love of God transforms lives and creates men and women who bear the fruit of the Spirit: "love, joy, peace, patience, kindness, goodness, faithfulness, gentleness, self-control; against such there is no law" (Gal. 5:22). He points out that if such characteristics are seen in their lives neither the law of China nor any other law will be able to overcome them. He himself exemplifies that spiritual truth.

On that second visit to China I also met other friends. One of them, a man in his 80s, once a great friend of the CIM, had written to me and now came to the airport to meet me. "Do you recognize me?" he asked. Later I spent hours in his home, meeting his family and other Christian friends.

Perhaps the most memorable moment of all was when the

door opened in another house where I was visiting and in came a white-haired man whom I had not seen for 30 years. Twenty years of prison and labor camp had left its mark on him, but his smile was radiant and his confidence in the Lord remained. Although he had had times of weakness, he said—when his faith faltered—I realized how deeply he had entered into the "fellowship of Christ's suffering."

I had other reunions with fellow workers. My joy was often tinged with sadness as I heard of their suffering, and of some who had given up their faith under great pressure.

I talked with one young man who had started a Bible study group in his home. His work situation gave him a fair amount of free time, so he would sit in his little hut, study the Scriptures and prepare Bible study materials. A year or two later the group had grown to 60 or 70 young people every week. They mimeographed the study materials and not only used them themselves but were able to get them to Christians in remote country areas. Two days' journey away they had discovered about 2,000 believers who had very few Bibles or study guides and who were delighted to receive the outlines and questions this young man prepared.

Opened Churches

In Guangzhou I asked our China International Travel Service guide if our group could go to a church. He knew about the Roman Catholic cathedral, which had been open only three weeks, and took us there early Sunday morning. About 100 Chinese and perhaps 50 or 60 foreigners were at the service, conducted in Latin with no singing or sermon. The Catholic Patriotic Association (CPA) still uses Latin for the mass, but in some places priests who have not joined the CPA use a Chinese liturgy.

God had a purpose in getting us to that service. I found myself sitting between a Chinese Christian and an African medical student. In the middle of the service, I saw the African pull out a Bible on which was written "Church of Uganda." Later he and his friend from Kenya came to my room and we had prayer and Bible study together. This was their first church service; they had not had any Christian fellowship for two years. I was able to introduce them to Chinese Christians after the Protestant service we also attended later that day.

In contrast to the cathedral, the Protestant service, held in a former Baptist church, was crowded with people. Almost every seat was taken. Hymns and Scripture readings were all printed on an order-of-service sheet, so everyone was able to take part. Many people were rejoicing in the opportunity to sing well-known hymns once again in public. But in addition to the older people with their memories of the past, there were many young people and even some children. I sensed deep devotion to the Lord in the service; a biblical message on "following Christ" was given by the pastor.

At the end of the service, I spoke to two men and a woman sitting behind me. She asked if I had any Bibles. One of the men said, "We have traveled for two days from another province to find out about this open church and to try to get some Bibles." I discovered that the older man in the group was formerly a member of a CIM church.

When one of my Christian friends from the past arranged a fellowship meeting for us in a home with a number of other believers, we heard an amazing story from our three new friends. They came from an area where there were tens of thousands of Christians and hundreds of house churches. In spite of severe persecution during the Cultural Revolution, great numbers of young people had believed.

Witness Amid Persecution

One of the three, a high school teacher, described a funeral service for an old pastor some years before that was attended by a large crowd of Christians. At that time they were not allowed to have any public meetings, but the young people determined that there should be a witness during the funeral service. They divided into groups, sang Christian hymns and made a large banner with the inscription "I am the resurrection and the life" (John 11:25) to carry in the funeral procession.

At the graveside an old man led in prayer. As soon as the funeral was over, he was arrested and sentenced to eight years in prison. Inquiries were made about who had written the words on the banner. In order to take the pressure off those who were being interrogated, the high school teacher who was telling us the story confessed to being the writer. He too was imprisoned. In her sorrow and distress his wife was comforted from the Scriptures by the words, "I am . . . the God of Abraham, the God of Isaac, and the God of Jacob" (Exod. 3:6) which led her to realize that this was also the God of her husband.

Meanwhile the young teacher in prison, feeling discouraged, began to sing the hymn, "The Way of the Cross I Will Follow." Another Christian prisoner heard the singing and was strengthened in faith. During the days that followed, people were converted in that prison and there were some remarkable answers to prayer.

After the worst testings of the Cultural Revolution had passed, the Church in this area continued to grow. Bible studies were started in different parts of the city, some meeting from four-thirty to six in the morning, others from six to eight A.M. Almost every day of the week some kind of meeting would be held, such as a special meeting on Tuesdays for training preachers. As many as 200 would attend one of the house-church communion services.

Among the hundreds of groups meeting in the countryside and neighboring towns, this teacher continued, there was a terrible shortage of Bibles. Many Christians had only handwritten copies of Scripture passages. Later, I was given a whole New Testament, one of many that were mimeographed after being copied by hand on wax stencils.

During this second journey, we visited the home of some secret Christians at the request of relatives in America. Having suffered greatly during the Cultural Revolution, these believers had maintained their faith but refrained from contact with other Christian groups. In the past they had experienced the questioning and trouble that could result.

We found a spirit of fear among some Christians, because of the years of suspicion and betrayal. Fellowship between Christians was hindered at times by a lack of trust in one another. On the other hand, some believers were extremely bold, feeling they had already suffered so much for the sake of Christ that it did not matter what happened to them in the future.

A few weeks after that 1979 visit, the Democracy Wall with its posters was closed, and during 1980 stronger measures were taken against those who supported dissidents as well as against intellectuals who criticized the Party. A young man was sentenced to eight years' imprisonment and five years' deprivation of political rights because he had openly put up posters appealing for support for a well-known dissident who had been imprisoned as a counterrevolutionary. Deng Xiaoping himself made a speech warning intellectuals not to be naive about the general tendencies and true aims of the so-called "democrats" and dissidents. He expressed the concern that party members and cadres, especially high-ranking cadres, must take a firm and clear-cut stand in this struggle saying it is absolutely impermissible to publicize any freedom of speech publication, assembly, or form of association which involves the counterrevolutionaries.

The more relaxed atmosphere, or the "Beijing Spring" as it has been called and which had lasted from November 1978 to December 1979, was over.

Nonetheless, in spite of restrictions, interest in religion was increasing. Especially in the countryside, the number attending the house churches was growing rapidly. In the cities hundreds of small groups met in homes. Roman Catholic churches were attracting large crowds, and crucifixes were being manufactured and sold on the street. This came to the attention of the Communist Youth League, who complained, "Selling religious objects in the marketplace is extremely injurious ideologically."[1]

The *China Youth News* gave its reason for that surge of spiritual response:

> Because their desires and aspirations in work, study, marriage, and cultural life cannot be met for the time being, some young people look to religion to lighten their sufferings. Others join religions because they like singing hymns or because they find it interesting to

pray to Buddha. In order to settle this problem, it is necessary to strengthen education and propaganda.[2]

Some government officials were clearly perturbed by the unexpected interest in religion.

An Unusual Book Exhibition

My wife Ruth accompanied me on my third visit to China in spring 1981. Opposition to the distribution of religious literature surfaced on that trip. Ruth and I traveled from Hong Kong to Shanghai on Operation Mobilization's ship, *M.V. Logos*. That ship was in essence a floating Christian book exhibition with a volunteer crew and staff from 25 countries. We had a great sense of expectancy and gratitude to God as we sailed up the Huang Pu River surrounded by ocean-going cargo ships, Chinese junks and sanpans.

But our first days in Shanghai were not easy. After the opening ceremony—attended by officials from Beijing and Shanghai—and the welcome to those invited to set up a book exhibition from the ship in the National Art Gallery in Beijing, we discovered that strict measures would be taken to insure that none of the literature on board was distributed among the people of Shanghai.

Before we arrived, a swarm of customs officials and soldiers came onto the ship. They went everywhere taking pictures, asking questions, especially among the 20 Chinese members of the crew, and listening to our meetings. We were informed that no books could be taken off the ship. The guards, who stayed on the ship 24 hours a day, often searched the bags of those going ashore.

We were allowed to take ashore a limited number of a brochure we had prepared for distribution, but in some places we heard that the police came around afterward and collected them from those who had received copies.

One of the officials who later traveled with us became very friendly and told me how impressed he was by the atmosphere on the ship and the friendliness of the crew members—a great contrast to what he had seen on other ships. He remarked on the simple life-style and the lack of luxurious accommodations, on the fact that the crew members and officers were all volunteers and on the absence of sexy pictures and other signs of immorality so prevalent on other ships that came into the port.

One team from the *Logos* went to Beijing to set up their exhibition. Seven hundred to 1,000 people attended each day. The books were displayed under various topics on shelves along the wall. Visitors exchanged their I.D. cards for books they could study but not take away, as no books were for sale. Among the secular books on display were two Bibles, Inter-Varsity Press's new *Illustrated Bible Dictionary* and about 30 other titles related to Christian issues.

I saw one student studying the Bible dictionary and Walter Trobisch's book, *I Married You*, was borrowed by a number of young people. A group who worked at a factory during the day and studied English at night told me how much they appreciated the opportunity to read these books.

The Growing Church

Again on this trip I was able to see a number of old friends. One who had been a leader in the China IVF group in 1948 (and who cannot be named here) wrote the following testimony in a letter:

> It is 33 years since we worshiped our God together. Through these years great changes have taken place in the world. Some Christians, including myself, have been restored and failed, then failed and were restored again. I should thank our heavenly Father. "All may change but Jesus never." He neither changes nor fails us. He loved and saved such a sinner like me in the past. Now he still loves and keeps me in his arms. He will love me forever! Whenever I thought of his eternal love, my eyes would be filled with tears—I left [the university] in early spring 1949. In that autumn I taught Chinese in a Bible College. Later I became a teacher in

a national school. During those years I went to the areas of minority nationalities many times. I lived and worked there with thousands of poor brothers and sisters in Christ. The pay from my teaching supported some fellow workers and myself. Sometimes we had only simple food to eat, but we have never been in want. At that time I wrote a hymn which says—

Daily manna given through barren land
Love so wondrous melts my heart
Feeding me each morn and night
Never failing in his grace.
Though my meals are plain and simple,
Great his loving grace to me.
Loudly sing Hallelujah
Until my life's work is done.

During the time when I suffered under the influence of the "Gang of Four" God often comforted me through this poem. Indeed his love is enough for me to enjoy.

The example and writing of this man have challenged countless Chinese students not only in China, but also in other Southeast Asian countries.

Wang Mingdao

One highlight of this third trip was when my wife and I visited Mr. and Mrs. Wang Mingdao.[3] This couple, beloved by Chinese Christians throughout the world, are known for their steadfast loyalty to the truth of the gospel.

During the Japanese occupation, Mr. Wang refused to allow his church in Beijing to become part of the religious organization set up by the occupying forces. In spite of threats he continued his fearless witness until the day of victory. From 1945 to 1949, he not only ministered to a large congregation in Beijing, but also spoke at conferences throughout the country. A prolific writer, he earned great respect because of his standards of righteousness and his condemnation of hypocrisy or compromise with evil on the part of Christians. He continued to be independent, not allowing his church to be associated with any outside organization. Although he had many friends among missionaries, he avoided links with foreign missions.

Mr. Wang strongly opposed liberal theological teaching and resolutely refused every invitation to join the Three-Self Patriotic Movement (TSPM). He insisted that he could have no fellowship with a movement whose leaders were known for theological liberalism, nor could his church take part in any political movement. He once said that he did not have a picture of Jesus in his church and he had no intention of putting up a picture of Chairman Mao.

After the first charges attacking his "reactionary thinking" and refusal to join the TSPM, Christian students started a "Stop Persecuting Wang Mingdao" movement. He continued preaching, and when no one dared to print his magazine he printed it on his own little hand-turned press. Finally in 1955 the government arrested him, together with many leaders in his church and in the student Christian fellowship.

During his first year of imprisonment, however, his mind and body were broken. He was forced to sign a confession and then was released. After that he went about saying, "I am Peter." When he was restored to physical and mental health, he went to the authorities, withdrew his confession and, as a result, was sent back to prison. He was released in early 1980, after a total of 23 years. All along he was bitterly attacked by the TSPM; its past and present leaders were among those who criticized him in 1955.

Soon after reaching Shanghai in 1981 we were invited to visit the Wang Mingdao home. His first words to me when we arrived were "Your hair is white." It had been over 30 years since I had been in his church for a student prayer conference held just before a large evangelistic campaign in Beijing. The messages he gave at that time were used to bring many students to faith in Christ.

Now he told us about his experiences in prison and sang some of the hymns that had sustained his faith. Though he might have been like Peter, he said, he had never been like Judas. He spoke at length about his concern for the Church and especially for young people. In a letter he said, "Many have good beginnings, but few have good endings." Always he urged young people to stand firm for the Lord.

While visiting another Christian home we were able to meet a doctor friend who was then in the city and who had prolonged his stay there in order to see me. He told of opportunities in the church where he worshiped, especially in leadership of the choir and how on some occasions he was able to visit house churches in other parts of the country. He arrived in one city, where we once worked, at nine in the evening to find a leaders' training session in progress. Immediately he was asked to teach, and so great was the hunger for the Word of God that they kept him talking until two A.M.

For me these personal contacts were evidence of the truth of reports that the Church was growing rapidly in many rural areas.

Another friend who has an important government position told me about the TSPM church in Shanghai. Although the great majority who attended the services were sincerely seeking to be fed with the Bread of Life, he expressed deep concern for the future of the Church because of the top leadership. Although TSPM churches were filled at every service, only a small proportion of Chinese Christians were to be found in those churches. Even greater numbers were still meeting in independent house groups at that time.

The same was true in the city of Hangzhou. Just after our arrival at the hotel, a tourist told us that he had come directly from a church where they were having choir practice. "If you go right away," he said, "you may be able to arrive before it finishes." So to our great joy we were able to meet with some of those Christians and learn a little bit of what God had been doing in that church.

Again we heard what was becoming a familiar story: although the church was crowded at every service, only a small proportion of the total number of the city's Christians would be found there. One of the pastors said they were trying to register the house groups so they could send people to help them. On a later visit we heard that another church was opened in the city, but large numbers still were meeting in homes and at that time had no wish to be associated with the TSPM. Having experienced the realities of prayer and the power of the Holy Spirit in their fellowships, their one concern was to build up the faith of new believers through the ministry of the Word of God.

The year 1981 thus was a good one for Christians; house churches were experiencing a great amount of freedom and their numbers were growing rapidly.

But for China as a whole, it proved to be a very difficult time. Considerable unrest existed throughout the country. Following the fall of Hua Guofeng at the end of 1980, the government faced an economic crisis. Many contracts with foreign firms were suspended. Up to 1 million workers were laid off. As unemployment increased, there was a rise in prices. For the first time people saw increases in salaries completely eaten up by inflation. That resulted in a wave of crime, especially in larger cities among unemployed youth.

Part of that unrest rose from the bitterness many young people felt as it became obvious that the evils of the Cultural Revolution could not be blamed on the Gang of Four alone. What had been obvious for some time was now admitted by the government: It was Mao's personal failure as a ruler that had caused so much distress to the whole nation. At the Sixth Plenum of the Communist Party held June 27-29, 1980, a document was issued containing the following statement:

> The Cultural Revolution which lasted from May 1966 to October 1976 was responsible for the most severe setbacks and the heaviest losses suffered by the Party since the founding of the People's Republic. It was initiated and led by Comrade Mao Zedong . . . the erroneous "left" theses on which he based himself . . . conformed neither to Marxism, Leninism, nor to Chinese reality. They represent an entirely erroneous appraisal of the prevailing class relations and political situation in the Party and state . . . . The Cultural Revolution did not in fact constitute a revolution or social progress in

any sense nor could it have possibly done so . . . it brought catastrophe to the Party, state, and the whole people.

No mention was made of the millions of people who died during the Cultural Revolution. Every effort was made to assure the people that, although Mao had made serious mistakes, his leadership had been essential for the success of the Revolution, and Mao Zedong Thought could never be discarded. But while the government tried to preserve Mao's image, the confidence of young people in the Party had been seriously undermined.

A Christian Tour Group

My fourth visit to China came later that same year, in September 1981, shortly after new leadership had been installed. Hu Yaobang was now chairman of the Chinese Communist Party. In an effort to maintain a low profile and to place younger men in top leadership positions, Deng Xiaoping was made head of the military commission. Zhao Ziyang became a vice-chairman and was designated premier. He and Chairman Hu now faced the tremendous task of leading China through the great changes that were bound to take place during the remaining years of the twentieth century.

I was leading a group of over 30 people, including five Chinese, four Canadians, four from England and one from Germany. They represented university and seminary professors, doctors and nurses, student workers, business people and other professionals.

We were often very conscious of God's leading, enabling us to meet with particular individuals. Once when traveling by plane I found myself sitting next to a Chinese surgeon and discovered that he was working in what had once been a very well-known mission hospital. He was not a Christian, but when I asked him if he knew any Christians he immediately replied, "Yes, I have one friend who is a very good Christian."

On the spur of the moment I asked if he would write his friend's name in my notebook. To my amazement he wrote down the name of a former fellow worker I had visited on a previous trip. When I told him this, he explained, "He is my brother-in-law—he has suffered greatly because he is a Christian."

A few days later I visited that friend. After years of suffering, he had been "rehabilitated" and was given a factory job. Most recently, following his retirement, he has become pastor of a city church.

It is hard to think of such meetings as just chance experiences. Does not God indeed answer the prayers of His servants when they seek for the direction of His Holy Spirit in all the contacts they make along the journey of life? I believe that His guiding hand brought to the hotel in Guangzhou the same African student whom I had met in the Roman Catholic cathedral on an earlier visit. He did not know that we were in China again, and we did not know at which hotel we would be staying for the last night of our tour. Just at the moment when I was in the lobby arranging room assignments for our group, he came in to post a letter. A few minutes earlier or later, and we would not have met; the opportunity for fellowship would have been lost. Such experiences indeed strengthen my faith in the loving care and overruling providence of our heavenly Father.

On this tour we were able to visit church services in Hangzhou and Nanjing and also meet with pastors of TSPM churches in Shanghai and Suzhou. In Hangzhou one of the pastors gave a gospel message on John 3:16. A pastor in another church that had just opened told us that there were probably half a million Christians in the province of Zhejiang alone. That was in contrast to the figure given by a TSPM leader in Shanghai, who told our group that Christians throughout the whole country numbered only 700,000 (that was also the official estimate of the number of baptized Christians in 1949). Since then the official estimate has been raised to 3 million.

In Shanghai our guide arranged for us to visit the community church, which had been visited by former President Jimmy Carter a few days before. The pastor spoke to our group in Chinese and I interpreted for him. The church did not have any Sunday School or young people's meetings, although Christian parents could bring their children to church. No meetings were allowed outside the church, but the pastor could visit sick members. One person in the church told us that any religious gathering in the home must be confined to family members.

Nanjing and Criticism

Our next stop was Nanjing, and here we encountered the most tension between the TSPM and house churches. A group of house-church Christians was waiting at the railway station to meet a member of our party. Shortly after we left to go to our hotel, they were detained and questioned by the police.

It was also obvious that our tour guide had been ordered to keep a close check on us; he was quite upset when two members of our group went off on their own the next day. They were able to spend time with one old pastor and learned that the six house churches in the city had been ordered to close and send their people to the TSPM church. The old pastor said, "Almost all the members of the choir in the open [TSPM] church come from my church."

Small meetings during the week were still held, although the pastor was often warned. Later we heard that this old man had been evicted from his home and, shortly afterward, he went to be with the Lord. Some members of his church continued to minister to groups in rural areas.

While in Nanjing we were able to visit the Nanjing Theological Seminary; I had made an appointment with a member of the faculty whom I had met in America. At the seminary we were warmly greeted by my friend. After talking to us about the seminary's history, however, our host went on to point out that there were misunderstandings between the Church outside China and the TSPM. He had heard about articles that I and others had written that were unfavorable toward the TSPM. He strongly objected to people praying for the TSPM as if something was wrong with it—"A person who is well," he said, "never likes to be prayed for as if he were sick." He therefore spoke strongly to me about what he described as my lack of understanding and sin against the Chinese Church.

Obviously, those who in any way criticize the TSPM are considered unfriendly, and because of that we face a serious problem. Some house-church leaders, who have undergone persecution for failing to join the TSPM, ask that Christians outside be made aware of the facts of their experience and not just listen to TSPM reports. The TSPM, however, regards itself as the only organization qualified to speak for Christians in China and deeply resents any criticism from the outside. It especially resents any suggestion that there is division between itself and the house churches.

Clearly, it is difficult for Western Christians to understand every aspect of the situation in China. We certainly have no desire to criticize the Church in China or to encourage division. We are, however, responsible to seek the facts: Some Christians attend the TSPM church, others attend independent house churches and still others are not connected with any church. Because we want to be "speaking the truth in love" (Eph. 4:15), we cannot just repeat TSPM statements. Many believers inside China who have no way of making their voice heard in other countries have urged us to give objective reports of both the TSPM and of the churches that remain independent.

The fact that we point out the fears that many Chinese Christians have about TSPM control of the Church does not indicate that we are "enemies of the New China." But, regrettably, it does mean that the political leaders of TSPM will brand us as unfriendly. At the same time, great numbers of Chinese Christians appreciate the love that motivates reports describing the situation of those with no official voice.

A Medical Team

Over a year passed before I was able to make a fifth trip to China, this time again with my wife, and back to the province of Henan. It was just over 40 years after our first term of service there. As Ruth and I came to the railway station in Zhengzhou, we were reminded of the several days' journey in 1941 with our baby as we crossed from free China into Japanese-occupied territory. Those were dangerous times, and we had rejoiced in God's guidance and protection on the road. Now in 1982 we arrived at the station to a welcome by government officials. Later I found myself sitting on a platform with four American Christian doctors at the opening ceremony of a seminar on cancer.

This had all begun just over a year before. On that trip Ruth and I had been walking along a road in Beijing when suddenly I heard a voice behind me saying to someone else, "Do you know David Adeney?" Turning around, I said, "I am he"—and was immediately embraced by a friend whom I had known as a medical student in 1950. He had heard I was there, had come to Beijing to look for me, and had just gotten off a bus as we came out of a restaurant.

During years of suffering, he said, God had kept him true to the faith. At times it seemed impossible to think of the Church in China surviving that strong persecution. Looking back over history it is easy to say, "The blood of the martyrs is the seed of the Church," forgetting that persecution is tremendously costly. Believers suffer terribly. There are casualties of faith and the sadness of betrayal.

My friend had been through all kinds of suffering including doing field labor, pulling weeds and dislodging stones from a barren plot of land. To him, it had seemed as if the Lord were saying, "What you are doing now is a picture of what I am doing in my Church. You are preparing this piece of land for harvest. I am preparing my Church for a spiritual harvest."

That harvest had now come. Hundreds of thousands of country people in Henan province had received the seed of the Word of God and entered into new life in Christ.

This doctor friend had gotten permission from his hospital to visit Beijing and to invite me to arrange for a team of American doctors to conduct a seminar on cancer. So a team of four Christian doctors was organized and now, together with some of their family members, they had arrived in Zhengzhou. The Henan Medical Association provided for all travel and hotel expenses in China, including a short stay in Beijing and visits to historical places of interest in other parts of Henan. Two hundred doctors from all over China had come to the seminar, many of them with much experience in cancer research.

As leader of the group, I was asked to give a short speech at the opening ceremony. I, of course, could not speak on scientific topics, but I did talk about "Whole Person Medicine." Mentioning the importance of good relations between doctor and patient, I used as an example the current slogan, "Five Emphases and Four Beautifuls,"[4] in which there was reference to emphasizing virtue and to the need for a beautiful spirit. Such characteristics are essential in the doctor's attitude, I said. Finally I described Christian doctors as being motivated by the compassion seen in the life of the Lord Jesus.

At a second half-day seminar in another city, when I gave a similar talk, it was interesting to see the faces of some of the local doctors light up when I mentioned the name of Christ. One Christian doctor spoke to me on the stairway; another ran out to the car, saying that she too was a believer. However, although the government was most generous in its hospitality, it was made quite clear that we were not permitted to have contact with Christians. Later we were told that Christians had come to watch us going in and out of the hospital, but they knew they could not come to see us.

One Sunday we were taken to Kaifeng, a city rich in relics of China's ancient history, where the CIM formerly had a hospital. Before going sightseeing we were able to worship in the church which had been opened by the TSPM and were impressed by the pastor's message on Revelation 11:1, "Rise and measure the temple of God and the altar and those who worship there." He brought into the pulpit a measuring rod, a winnowing basket and pictures he had drawn, illustrating the various kinds of Christians to be found in the church. Later I was able to speak with him for a few minutes.

As we drove along the country roads of Henan with their crowds of donkeys, mule carts, bicycles and country folk carrying heavy burdens, I was reminded of my long cycle rides during the years when Ruth and I worked in the towns and villages of Henan. Now as we watched the farmers on the threshing floors, we thought of the spiritual harvest also being reaped.

Right at the end of the Cultural Revolution, in 1976, there was serious persecution in Henan. Authorities were concerned at the increasing number of home churches, and in one area three followers of the Gang of Four were appointed to destroy the growing Christian community. Three of the church leaders were imprisoned, and night after night Christians were interrogated and beaten.

Then, changes began to take place. Prime Minister Zhou Enlai died, and a few months later Mao Zedong himself died. Following the arrest of the Gang of Four, the three responsible for persecuting the Henan Christians found themselves also in prison. One was placed in the same cell as one of the Christian leaders, and there he too came to know Christ. When Christians were released from prison in 1979, they were welcomed by tens of thousands of other believers.

As we traveled through the villages we heard that members of the Public Security Bureau (PSB) had said, "There are Christians in every village" and that a government report referred to 1 million new believers in Henan. Such statements were in sharp contrast to the official word given us in a country commune. It was a well-run commune, close to the city, and with a high standard of living. One of the doctors asked if there were any Christians there. The spokeswoman looked rather confused, said no, and then turned to the local official representative (cadre) who was accompanying us. Immediately he confirmed her words: "Christians are all in the towns—you won't find them in the country."

That was far from the truth. One of my friends visiting a town in Henan met an old pastor who lived in a small two-room house with his son and daughter-in-law. The Sunday morning service was held in the courtyard, and many came at 6:30 A.M. hoping to get seats for the 8:30 service. On that particular Sunday the pastor was not at the service; he was out in the villages baptizing 114 new believers. Speaking about what was happening, he repeatedly said, "We are not doing anything; it is God who is working in China today." In one county of this province, 70 percent of the people are Christians. During 1981, 300 were baptized in the town where we formerly lived, and over 100 young people have gone out to spread the gospel in other areas.

Soon after the morning service in Kaifeng we visited a museum. While we were there, one of the young cadres from the local office responsible for receiving visitors came and sat beside me. "I've recently been through a very traumatic experience," he said. "My grandmother has just died. She was very religious and went to church every Sunday. I used to laugh at her, but she always told me that Sunday was the happiest day of the week for her."

"I share your grandmother's faith," I replied.

"I know," he said. "These doctors are scientists, and you are a philosopher [!], yet you all believe in God. I can't understand it." For a few minutes I was able to tell him why I believed in God.

Undoubtedly many Chinese were impressed by the lives and attitudes of the doctors on our team. One of our tour guides mentioned what a favorable impression their friendliness and humility had made on the other doctors they met. A scroll that was presented to us with the words, "Friendship endures forever," perhaps sums up one of the main benefits arising from Christian participation in such cultural and educational exchanges: Friendships are formed, and prejudices concerning Christianity are dispelled.

Visiting Universities

When I visited China again in 1984 I traveled with just one other friend and stayed in university hostels provided for foreign experts. One Sunday I was able to speak to about 70 members of the foreign community in Beijing at their weekly service. Many do not understand Chinese, although increasing numbers are studying the language. In Beijing there is no lack of Christian fellowship, since among the hundreds of foreigners working in the embassies, studying or teaching in the universities or engaged in business are many members of the household of God.

It was springtime in Beijing, shortly before the arrival of

President Ronald Reagan. The cold winds of the Anti-Spiritual Pollution Campaign (see chapter 4) were beginning to die down. Nonetheless, a Chinese Christian friend told me that attendance at their weekly meeting for prayer and fasting, which had been held in different homes, was decreasing because of stricter government control over house meetings. A number of people had been arrested and others were afraid to come.

Grounds for arrest included: (1) receiving religious literature from abroad, (2) "pushing the gospel," which meant active witness for Christ in public places outside registered church buildings and (3) opposition to the TSPM. Those arrested would be given a further period of political training and then, if they had a good attitude and agreed to join the TSPM, they would be released.

Christians now active in the government-approved churches say little about persecution. One friend, whose father I had known very well, invited me to her home, telling me she had obtained special permission from the head of the neighborhood committee to do so. We talked freely about the past, and I saw a picture album of her family. During the Cultural Revolution the husband and wife were separated for 18 years, when the husband, a teacher, was imprisoned in the school with other "reactionary" teachers. They were beaten by students and forced to do hard labor. Now they have been reinstated professionally, and the husband has a good teaching position. For them there is no longer persecution—because they attend the TSPM church.

Christians I met on this sixth journey came from different backgrounds. Similarly, some were members of the TSPM church, while others worshiped secretly in their homes. There was little contact between the two groups; some regretted the lack of trust that caused separation between groups of believers.

Medical Advances

My seventh journey to China in June 1985 with a team of

Christian doctors and nurses from America and New Zealand revealed striking contrasts. China has indeed made progress in the field of medical services. We saw well-equipped hospitals in the big cities where advanced medicine is being practiced. Members of our team gave lectures and performed operations in the Sixth People's Hospital in Shanghai which was formerly the China Inland Mission headquarters and hospital. In recent years it has gained an international reputation for its work in the field of restoring severed limbs and restructuring the hand.

But, part of our time was spent in smaller places not fully open to tourists. In these towns we saw hospitals lacking the most basic medical equipment serving large populations. We had two long car journeys through the countryside and noticed the many new buildings in the villages. Obviously, the people are more prosperous than in the past, but still there is little mechanization in agriculture and the farmers spend long days of backbreaking work in the rice fields.

A group of young doctors told us that after a five-year course in medical college they receive only 60 RMB (just over $20.00 U.S.) a month. They said that today many country farmers can make more money than they do. They feel that while the standard of living has greatly improved in rural areas near the cities, the situation for young intellectuals is discouraging. Young people must depend upon their parents' income because the older people get higher salaries. At the same time the cost of living is increasing.

In the larger cities there is, however, a greater sense of freedom. Some of the young people have the opportunity to choose the work they want to do. They can travel freely but must register when they stay in another place and cannot work except where they are domiciled. People are excited about the progress being made and everyone is seeking to obtain the "four big things"—a television, a tape recorder, a washing machine and an electric fan.

The situation for Christians still seems very complex. A church pastor spoke of the amazing things that God is doing. Over 1,200 attend his early Sunday service and 400 come to the second one. He said that, while in some churches there is tension between different types of pastors, in his church all three church workers come from the same background. Hundreds come to Bible study during the week.

He spoke especially of the spiritual hunger among the old people. Shanghai has 1 million over 60 years of age. After retirement they have little to do. Many suffered during the Cultural Revolution. Old values have been destroyed, and a spiritual hunger exists which needs to be filled with the gospel of Christ.

Outwardly there is full freedom to go to the churches. Many faithfully preach the gospel. But we were repeatedly told that the Church is controlled by the government and that some of the pastors are government agents who have little to contribute to the spiritual needs of the people. A friend who traveled a long way in order to meet us told us of one area which he visited. Before Liberation there were only 2,000 Christians. Now there are 20,000 and 320 meeting places. The Church in that area illustrates the problems that Christians sometimes face.

The pastor in one place had no message and preached only 15 or 20 minutes a Sunday. But the people would come hours before the service. During that time they would practice hymns, learning from handwritten posters, and then an old brother would lead them in Bible study. All of this took place before the formal service started.

We also met Christians who do not go to any church. One university teacher told us that it was not convenient for him to go to church. He has Bible study in his home, and his grown-up son, who also holds a responsible position in the academic world, is now growing in the Lord. He has been greatly helped by American Christian English teachers.

Some Christians avoid the Church because of their knowledge of the government's control. They feel it is impossible to "serve two masters." Others remain secret believers fearing that they would lose their academic position or at least could be barred from promotion.

Through our contact with Christians from various backgrounds, we could clearly see that religious freedom is definitely limited. Some Christians are making an active contribution to the building up of their country but, in some cases, they face discrimination because of their faith. We rejoiced to hear of increasing numbers of people attending church services, but we also sympathized with the concern of some that the spiritual vitality of the Church could easily be diluted and evangelistic outreach hindered.

Some feel that despite restrictions and the subtle growing demand that "Caesar" should have the preeminence, they can still witness within the government framework. Others however feel that their Christian brothers and sisters within the organized Church are being subtly affected by the political influences. So they determine to keep entirely separate from an organization which they feel must eventually cause its leaders to compromise in their faith.

This journey enabled us to understand some of the tensions under which Christians live in China and challenged us to enter more deeply through prayer into the spiritual conflict of which we saw only a very small part. As members of the Kingdom of God we can never be satisfied till the love of our Lord Jesus is made known to this great people. There was so much that we could love and appreciate but also there was evidence of much sorrow and frustration.

To these hardworking people there surely must come the opportunity to hear the Saviour's words, "Come unto me, all ye that labour and are heavy laden and I will give you rest" (Matt. 11:28, *KJV*).

As I look back on photographs from these seven recent journeys to China, I realize that the Chinese situation can never be pictured with a still camera. Such pictures reflect only one time and one place, for the situation is always changing. Any particular circumstance must be seen in the context of a broader panorama.

What is happening in China today is inseparably linked not only with the Revolution of 1949, but with thousands of years of Chinese history and culture. But while China changes and uncertainty characterizes all future predictions, the Rock on which the Church is built never changes. In a Church that has come forth stronger than ever after the terrible upheavals of the past three decades, we see some of the undying principles of the Word of God.

3

PROGRESS AND PROBLEMS

The most obvious changes in China today are those seen by tourists in the large cities and nearby villages, where living standards are obviously higher than in the past. China is proud of the progress made during recent years. Every village work unit visited by tourists tells the story of the improvement in production and standard of living since 1949. It is impressive to hear of greatly improved medical facilities, progress in the fight against illiteracy, increase of roads and railways, and the gradual introduction of mechanization in agriculture.

The growth of many new industries, changes in methods of education and building programs in many cities also point to the progress taking place in China. Markets are crowded with a great variety of produce. In the cities the drab look of the past is changing; dress styles are more attractive. As in the 1930s, Shanghai continues to set the fashion trend. Young men in Western-style suits and ties are becoming a familiar sight. Makeup is increasingly being used by younger women. But at the same time, undesirable elements in Western society are again causing problems.

Just a few years ago, in 1979, the prevalent impression was still of the backwardness of society. The *People's Daily* at that time carried the following evaluation.

> In China today there are a hundred broken things to be
> mended and a hundred tasks to be accomplished . . . .
> China's economy at present is very backward. For the
> time being it is unlikely that there will be big advances
> in living standards. We must tell the people the truth
> about the situation.[1]

Yet even since that reference to a "hundred broken things"
China's progress has been remarkable, although tremendous
problems remain. Inequalities and low standards of living contribute to what has been called the "revolution of rising expecta-
tions" brought about by a growing knowledge of the outside
world through radio, TV and contacts with overseas Chinese
and Westerners.

Now, since the rise to power of Deng Xiaoping in 1978,
China has embarked on a massive program of modernization.
Under the slogan of the "Four Modernizations" the Chinese
Communist Party (CCP) has sought to mobilize the entire country to update the key areas of *agriculture, industry, science and
technology* and *national defense* (in that order). This program has
continued to be the pervading domestic policy of the 1980s.

Christians concerned that the gospel should bring wholeness
to those who are broken in body, mind and spirit will respond to
Paul's injunction to pray for rulers and for all people (see 1 Tim.
2:1-2). Thus, Chinese Christians are concerned not only with
their own personal problems, but also with the impact of their
lives on their society and nation. As farmers, health workers,
engineers, secretaries or whatever, they long to have a benefi-
cent influence on friends, neighbors and colleagues—spiritually
and otherwise.

Love for the Church of Jesus Christ and for the people of
China calls us to be concerned about both their material and spiritual needs. That requires our attempting to identify not only
with their personal concerns, but also with those of their nation.
Only then can we pray effectively for the welfare of the over 1
billion Chinese and the rulers who are responsible for the stability of that society.

Even though their political leaders may propagate a militant atheism diametrically opposed to Christian belief, Christians ought not approach China with an anti-Communist attitude. Rather we are called to pray that the light of the glory of God may shine into the hearts of those blinded by the god of this world (see 2 Cor. 4:4), whatever their ideological background. They can be reached with the gospel only through humble, loving service. Communists who have long been prejudiced against Christians have been changed in their attitude when they see servants of Christ showing love and humility through their concern for the good of the people.

China's Problems Today

Population

Beside the road outside our guest house in 1982 were several colorful billboards picturing various types of Chinese people—a reminder to the townspeople that all must take part in the impending national census. Soon the papers announced that China has 1 billion, 8 million people. Even if statistics have little meaning to us, we can begin to grasp the immensity of such a figure if we realize that 1 billion minutes ago would take us back to the time of Christ. Twenty-five babies are born in China each minute. The outstanding impression in the minds of many visitors is the masses of people. In towns the streets are crowded. In rural areas, the fields, roads and markets are full of people.

Seven of China's 22 provinces have a population of over 50 million, making each of them more populous than most of the nations of the world (see population map). Sichuan, now above 100 million people, is more populous than any European country except the Soviet Union. Because deserts, mountains and grasslands make up 90 percent of China's land area, one-quarter of the world's population has to be fed from 7 percent of the world's arable land. And this area is decreasing as more and more agricultural land is taken for the building of houses. In 20 years the area under cultivation has fallen by 30 million acres. China's population has more than doubled during the 50 years

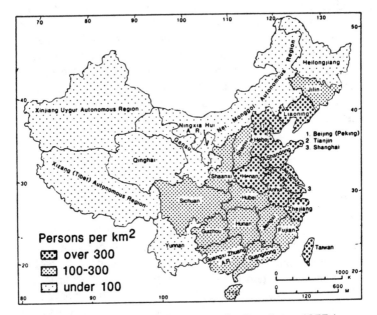

China's Population Distribution by Province, 1977.*

*C. W. Pennell and L. J. C. Ma, *China: The Geography of Development and Modernization*, Scripts Series in Geography, (London: Edward Arnold Publishers, Ltd., 1983), p. 105. Used by permission.

since I first arrived in Shanghai; half of the present population has been born since Ruth and I left China in 1950. The average age of the population is 26.[2]

China's present dilemma is partly due to Mao Zedong's unenlightened policy: "Things would be better done with more people." Mao believed that the masses of people were China's most valuable resource. Others disagreed, but Mao continued to give privileges to women with more children. That policy was popular in the countryside, since peasants wanted to have as many male children as possible to provide a larger labor pool for the family. What that meant in reality was that the amount of land available for each individual rapidly decreased. It is now recognized that China's population must be kept below 1 billion, 200 million by the end of the century if economic growth is not to be threatened.

As long ago as 1865, before the sailing of the *Lammermuir* with the first large group of CIM missionaries, Hudson Taylor constantly referred to China's vast population. He spoke of 380 million still waiting to hear the gospel and, after describing the death rate in China, he went on to say:

> Do you believe that each unit of these millions has an immortal soul? And that there is none other name under heaven whereby they must be saved? . . . It will not do to say that you have no special call to go to China. With these facts before you and the command of the Lord Jesus to go . . . you need rather to ascertain whether you have a special call to stay at home.[3]

We might not use the same language today in referring to the need in China, for we cannot appeal for missionaries to go from the West. But the spiritual need of millions without Christ and the biblical truth of salvation through Christ alone—those facts have not changed. So, like Hudson Taylor in his day, we too should be deeply concerned for a population that is almost three times greater than in 1865. What can we do to strengthen the Chinese Church that is responsible to reach this generation of its fellow countrymen?

When a governmental family-planning program of "one child per family" began, it had very little effect. The government then made its policy compulsory, imposing fines of 1,000 yuan ($357 U.S.), or more on those who had more than one child. For example, in 1982 our tour guide told us about a couple whose salaries were seriously reduced for a whole year because they had a second child. In early 1984, the daughter of a Beijing University administrator was heavily fined because she refused to have an abortion.

It has always been important in China to have a son to carry on the family name. When our first child, a daughter, was born in Henan, our friends "comforted" us with the thought that she could look after the little brothers who would follow! Now that peasants can cultivate their own land and raise crops for profit, it is even more important for them to have a son to work the land.

Sons are a form of old-age insurance. Country people naturally ask, "If we have only one daughter, who will support us in our old age?" How could a daughter, especially if she marries into another family and has her own child, support her aging parents as well? A Chinese newspaper, *Ming Bao*, on May 28, 1983, reported that millions of couples, especially in the rural areas, were ignoring the family-curtailment regulation.

As a result, in order to enforce the birth-control policy, compulsory sterilization campaigns have been carried out in some provinces. Mothers who have become pregnant for a second time have been forced to have abortions and submit to sterilization. Neighborhood committees or work units are given the responsibility of keeping check on each child-bearing family so that quotas for births in its district are not exceeded. In some work units, women's physiological charts are posted on the board.

We can only imagine the agony endured by young Christian women when forced to undergo an abortion. At the same time, both the official Catholic and Protestant churches are forbidden to express any objection to government-enforced abortions, since that would be regarded as interfering with the social system.

In some areas there is a serious imbalance between boys and

girls, and newspapers have reported the killing of girl babies, even though this is strongly condemned and prison sentences have been given to those convicted.[4] The birth-control policy is also creating social problems. A sole child who is exceedingly precious to the parents, and with no siblings to play and share with, may easily become spoiled. By March 1985 some exceptions to the one-child policy were being made in the countryside.

In spite of all its inherent difficulties, the strict birth-control policy has been partially effective recently, especially in the cities. The birth rate has been cut down. By July 1984 Shen Guoxiang of the state Family Planning Commission said that it had declined to 18.64 per thousand, from 24.2 in 1982 (*Wenhui Bao*, July 4, 1984).

Living Standards

Closely related to the population problem is the need to raise living standards for the 80 percent of the population who live in rural areas. As people learn more and more about the situation outside their own villages, they demand a higher standard of living. The contrast between countryside and town is still vast. Those living in cities have more access to consumer goods, more entertainment and more attractive jobs. Because of that, they tend to look down on the peasants who spend their days working in the fields. The hopes of country people were raised at the time of the Revolution when they received land from the landlords and, for a time, they worked very hard on this newly acquired land.

When Mao set up the commune system in 1958 it was supposed to solve all the rural people's problems. "Setting up a people's commune is like going to heaven—the achievements of a single night surpass those of several millennia." Mao's objective was to destroy the "Three Great Differences": between those doing mental and physical labor, between workers and peasants and between urban and rural inhabitants. The income of educated people was not to rise faster than that of peasants. To accomplish that goal, millions of educated young people from the cities were sent to the countryside.

The peasants' duty was to build socialism and to work for the commune rather than for themselves. Countless political meetings were held to make sure Mao's ideology was followed. At the same time, they were given the "Five Guarantees": food, clothing, fuel, education of children and proper burial. There was little incentive to work hard to increase production. The commune was to be one large family, and everybody was to *chi da guo fan* (eat out of the same large pot).

Very soon, however, there was discontent. Because the huge communes proved unwieldy, in the early '60s they were reduced in size and their number trebled. Still, there was little incentive for the peasants to work hard. Many felt they were not working for themselves but for the privileged class of the Party elite. Even during the Cultural Revolution Deng Xiaoping advocated the providing of incentives for labor. That idea was, however, strongly opposed by Mao who insisted that there should be guaranteed jobs and fixed wages.

Since the fall of the Gang of Four, Mao's policy has been completely reversed. It became clear that although the commune system may have succeeded as an instrument of political control, economically it was a disaster. Formerly the Dazhai Commune was the great example of agricultural progress. But when its statistics were finally disclosed to be grossly inflated, the *Beijing Review* remarked that it was important "to learn from Dazhai by negative example."

At the present time, ability to produce rather than "socialist purity" is the measure of success. By the mid-1980s communes had been dismantled. The land was divided into small plots and contracted out to be farmed privately. Under this Agricultural Responsibility System, the peasant pays both a small rent and an agricultural tax and must sell a fixed annual quota of grain to the government at a controlled price. Excess production can be retained or sold, and vegetables and other produce can be freely traded. Thus peasants are able to make a profit, and as a result are showing much greater initiative.

All observers agree that the improvement in real rural standards of living in the past four years, whether in fact a doubling of income or not, represents an improvement of far greater magnitude than occurred during the entire period from 1952 to 1977.[5]

Thus, the commune as a political system has been abolished. Townships are now the center of local rural government, with villages as the next lower tier in the system and households (families) as the basic unit.

At the same time, peasants are encouraged to develop rural industries and small businesses.[6] Formerly, farmers were afraid to be known as "rich peasants," but now those who do well and make money are praised as "model workers." On the surface, the trend is to encourage money-making, and peasants and workers have taken full advantage of this. Frequent reports in the Chinese press highlight the "rags to riches" stories of enterprising individuals who have made large sums by dint of hard work and entrepreneurial skills.[7]

On the other hand, decollectivization in the rural areas is also leading to new problems. The country people are becoming more independent and are less easily controlled than previously. A new road to success has opened up—not through politics, as in the past, but through becoming wealthy. People are inspired by self-interest rather than by political idealism, and the government is becoming concerned about mercenary tendencies, especially as these lead to an increase in crime. Throughout 1983 and 1984 newspapers have often contained accounts of economic crime and corruption.[8] Stealing is far more prevalent than in the past. Examples of widespread petty dishonesty are seen in the frequent instances of conductors on Beijing's crowded buses engaging in heated confrontations with passengers who have not paid for a ticket.

Worse still are the questions raised by some observers as to whether or not China is in fact turning capitalist. Those questions are all the more valid in light of the fact that the agricultural reforms have been paralleled by similar shifts in the urban/industrial sector, and workers there are jumping on the "get rich quick" bandwagon. As time has gone on, fear has grown that the new opportunities will be abused. Within the Party itself there are still conservative left-wing factions who oppose Deng's policies, and he himself has warned that making money is not an end in itself.

> We advocate that some regions get rich first, so that they can help the backward areas develop better, and not create two class divisions. Advocating that some people get rich first has the same rationale, so that they can help those who are not rich become rich as well.[9]

In 1979 I visited peasant homes near the cities, which were obviously showplaces for tourists. They had color TVs and other electronic equipment, and their owners spoke enthusiastically of the great improvement in living standards. However, when Ruth and I were in Henan in 1982, we noticed the contrast between the communes close to the large urban areas and communes off the beaten track. Once, when our bus stopped in a rural area, I was able to look into a village in which conditions seemed to be similar to those we had known over 40 years ago.

Although it is true that living conditions have improved in many areas, statistics are not always reliable. More realistic reports indicate that there is more poverty in some areas of the country than would appear from the glowing accounts given to visitors. In 1979 a farm director in Northwest China was quoted by a Chinese newspaper:

> The peasants here are poverty stricken. Since 1959 one political movement after another was launched in our villages, and with each the peasants' lives became a little more intolerable.[10]

In 1980 the *People's Daily* said that 100 million peasants had drawn no benefit from collectivization and were still as poor as in 1949, needing state assistance to survive. One Chinese in eight in 1980 was permanently hungry, and throughout the country the supply of grain and cotton cloth for rural inhabitants had not increased since 1957.[11]

In 1979, poverty-stricken people appeared in Beijing carrying banners and chanting, "We want food! We want clothing! Down with oppression!" In 1983 about 50 beggars staged a demonstration at Datong railway station in Shanxi province, demanding a free train ride to Beijing to make their needs known.[12]

At the same time, 1983 was one of the best years since the Revolution. The total grain output was 380 million tons, 26 million more than in the previous year.[13] Some farmers are now earning more than people in the cities.[14] A Beijing university professor earns considerably less than many prosperous farmers. The government has done a great deal to improve the distribution of food so that, even in remote areas where the harvest may have failed and there is still great poverty, widespread starvation may be prevented. In the cities, food seems to be abundant although beggars are still visible.

As some peasants become rich through the setting up of rural industries, others are dissatisfied. The newspapers reported that a peasant from Anhui province pinned a note to the door of a government office saying, "While I borrow one bowl of grain after another, I sink deeper and deeper into debt." As the gap widens between rich peasants and the very poor, it is not surprising that there are protests. The average rural income today for the whole country is just over $120 a year (U.S.), compared with $210 (U.S.) for urban residents.[15] By comparison some cadres, ex-cadres, demobilized soldiers and graduate students, who have set up rural enterprises, have a much higher income.

> The most startling contrast is seen in Shenzhen near Hong Kong, where some household incomes run as high as $9,000 (U.S.). Nine hundred factories and office buildings are used in the production of products as diverse as Cabbage Patch dolls, portable telephones and color television sets. The latest slogan "Time is money" was severely criticized by some senior Communist Party members who described it as "capitalistic rubbish."[16]

Charges that the present economic policies are reviving capitalism and betraying the Marxist principles on which the new Chinese society is built have been strongly refuted by present government leaders. An article in *People's Daily* of December 7, 1984 states, "We cannot expect the works of Marx and Lenin in their day to solve our modern problems."

Perhaps foreseeing the way in which the international press would hail such an admission as the beginning of the downfall of Marxism, the *People's Daily* made a small correction the next day. It said that the sentence should have read "to solve *all the problems of today.*" The original article had indeed urged persistent study of Marxism and the obligation to "enrich and develop it in our practice." It said that Marxist teaching must not be allowed to hinder economic development, but it still remains as the ideological foundation for Chinese socialist society.

A few days after the statement concerning Marxism, the *Liberation Army Daily* warned against any lessening of Party discipline and ideological purity. So it is quite clear that there has not been any total repudiation of Marxism, since that would question the Party's own legitimacy. Rather, the Chinese government was emphasizing that "clinging to every jot and tittle of Marxist dogma is infantile and can not help China in her great task of modernization." That is in line with CCP Chairman Hu Yaobang's call to integrate the basic tenets of Marxism with modern conditions.

Up until Mao's death in 1976 there was no inflation. Everyone had to have ration coupons—as they still do—and if anyone wanted any "luxuries" they had to get special tickets from their units. In recent years, however, free markets have been introduced and the country people are able to sell their vegetables at prices higher than government prices. Because the cost of living has begun to increase and salaries have not kept up, many are concerned about the danger of inflation. This is more of a problem in the cities than in the countryside. In May 1984 Premier Zhao Ziyang gave an impressive report of the progress in living standards during the past year. The average per capita income of the peasants rose 14.7 percent; urban income was up 15.5 percent.

Increased wealth brings new problems. With the growing

emphasis on materialism, even Christians are reportedly tempted to take part in the struggle to obtain material possessions, even through illegal or dishonest means.

Recently, the Agricultural Responsibility System, formerly so successfully implemented in the countryside, is being used in the cities to stimulate initiative among people working in factories and small businesses.

Housing Shortage

With its rapid population growth, China faces an acute shortage of housing, especially in the large cities. In 1978, there were only 3.6 square meters per person, a 20 percent decrease in living space since 1949.[17] Older homes that formerly housed two or three families now may have numerous families each living in one room. As a result, house-churches have found it quite difficult to obtain adequate space for large meetings. In the countryside, where houses are often larger, courtyards covered with a mat roofing can accommodate hundreds of people.

Visitors to Beijing are impressed by the mushrooming of high-rise apartment buildings every year. I was invited to a meal in the home of an old friend and, after climbing to the fourth floor, was entertained in the living room of a very small, but nicely furnished apartment. It was a great contrast to a home I had visited in another city, where my friend with his wife and new baby lived in one dark room with no outside window and only a single door leading to a dark hallway.

It is encouraging to see that some progress has been made in finding improved living quarters for intellectuals. When I first visited a professor who had been turned out of his home during the Cultural Revolution, he and several members of his family were living in two small rooms. The bedroom was completely filled with beds, and the toilet was only a hole in the floor. Now he has been moved into a more spacious apartment with several bedrooms, a bathroom, a kitchen and a small veranda.

There are long waiting lists for new apartments, however, and it has been said that in no section of society is there so much corruption as in the housing industry. Some highly placed cadres may possess several apartments, while others who have no influential friends to help them wait for years to obtain a suitable home. Much housing is provided by the work unit. If the work unit is prosperous, accommodations may be good, but those who belong to work units with less prestige may have to wait a very long time before receiving something suitable.

In the more prosperous villages near the cities, country people are building their own houses. Consequently the contrast is striking between homes in well-to-do rural communities and those in more remote villages. Many country houses are no different now than they were hundreds of years ago.

Land use—the balance between space for housing and for cultivation—is a critical issue especially in rural areas.[18] Although peasants may gradually accumulate sufficient funds to begin construction of new homes, overall planning may preclude individual families from building on land that has been assigned for crops. An example of this is the problem faced by the Evergreen Commune outside Beijing. This commune is trying to preserve its 2,560 intensively farmed hectares (one hectare = 2.47 acres), largely devoted to providing for the capital's consumption, in face of housing needs for its 13,000 families.

Another problem faced by would-be builders, both in cities and countryside, is the lack of materials. Lack of skilled labor is also a major constraint in the rural building boom. The government has responded by launching a massive program to teach basic building methods in which 114,000 peasants were trained in 1982.

Officials also realize that long-term housing solutions depend on improved water and energy supplies. Their aim, therefore, is to close the gap between the more prosperous areas of eastern China and the impoverished interior—especially Shanxi and Shaanxi provinces—where mud-thatched cottages and even cave dwellings are still common. To as great an extent as possible, those ambitious goals will have to be achieved by privately accumulated savings and the spare-time labor of the residents themselves.

Improved standards of housing are thus the result of adjustments now being made to the Chinese economic structure.

Between 1980 and 1984, total new housing built in China has been estimated at 2 billion square meters—which is equivalent to all such building in the previous two decades. Greater flexibility for local enterprise, increased incentives for the production of materials formerly in short supply and greater amounts of discretionary income at the disposal of families all add up to an optimistic outlook for China's housing picture in the remaining years of this century.

Education

Improvement of living standards depends also on progress in the field of education. China has done a great deal to overcome the problem of illiteracy, but government reports refer to 200 million who are illiterate or semiliterate (see Fig. 1).

Illiterates and Semiliterates in 1984

- 22.9% of those aged 12 and above
- 45% of women
- 31.9% of total population
  (contrast with 52.4% in 1954)[19]

Figure 1

The low level of education in the rural areas naturally affects church growth. In some areas large numbers have become Christians by experiencing healing in answer to prayer, but the shortage of teachers and literature suitable for semiliterates may result in a lack of understanding of the basic truths of the gospel. The importance of elementary gospel radio programs for country people is obvious.

At the beginning of 1984, nearly 200 million people, or onefifth of the population, were receiving various forms of regular education.

Education in 1984

- 11.4 million in preschool classes
- 136 million in primary school (43.9% female)
- 46.3 million in secondary school (39.6% female)
- 1.2 million college students (24.4% female)
- 36,000 post-graduate students[20]

Figure 2

The statistics in Fig. 2 are impressive when compared with statistics just prior to the Cultural Revolution. For example, four times as many students are in middle schools today as were in 1966.

But it is not enough to have children in school. There must also be capable teachers. In the province of Guizhou, the poor quality of primary and middle-school teachers was blamed for the failure rate among students. In October 1983, three-quarters of the school teachers in that province took an exam. Only one-eighth of the primary and one-quarter of the secondary teachers passed.[21]

In the whole country only one-third of the primary school students will reach secondary school. Less than 1 percent will make it to college, compared with 25 percent in developed countries. By 1990, however, it is planned to double the number in higher education as well as multiply by five the students in extension programs though TV courses, night school and correspondence courses.[22]

The balance is also tipped in favor of city over countryside. The new incentives to peasants to increase production have increased pressures on families to pull their children out of school early, or not to send them at all. In the cities, academic competition, as in many Asian countries, is beginning to intensify. Selection of promising youngsters begins early and the pupils are chosen sometimes even from kindergarten to attend "key" schools that offer them the chance of becoming one of the 1.7 million students permitted to take the national college entrance exams.[23]

Education is still closely related to the ideological goals of the Communist Party. It must again be emphasized that Marxism has not been abandoned, although aspects of it are considered irrelevant to the needs of today's world. Education is still based on Marxist thought—e.g., history is taught within a completely Marxist framework. In one school I visited, the spokeswoman for the administration emphasized the fact that the whole philosophy of education was based on the teachings of Marx, Lenin and Mao Zedong. Children are expected to join the Young Pioneers, and students in their teens are urged to become members of the Communist Youth League, which is stronger in the cities than in rural areas. In both organizations there is strong atheistic teaching. A Chinese Christian teaching in a teacher training college told me that if the authorities had reason to believe he was a Christian, and knew he was influencing his students, he would be in serious trouble.

Lack of Higher Education In Science and Technology

A university education is greatly sought after and competition is intense for the few available places. College graduates can expect to get both better salaries and more meaningful work. The government hopes to double the number of university students by 1990, requiring significant expansion of China's 700 universities, colleges and teaching institutions.[24]

China's leaders blame the country's primitive state of economic development on the backwardness of its science and technology, recognizing that a main reason for this was the persecution of intellectuals during the Cultural Revolution.[25] When Mao referred to intellectuals as "the stinking ninth class," some people may have recalled the words of the Chinese sage, Mencius:

"Those who use their minds rule; those who use their muscles are ruled." Even today many of the older leaders in government feel threatened by the possible rise of an elite intellectual class.

Under Deng Xiaoping's leadership, however, intellectual qualifications and not just political reliability are essential for government positions, at least at lower levels. Deng, in his rehabilitation of the educational establishment, denies Mao's claim that intellectuals are essentially bourgeois. Rather, he affirms that people who work with their minds are just as much laborers as those who engage in physical activity.

The number of scientists and technicians has greatly increased; there are almost 100 times more than in 1949. Yet such a demand still exists for highly trained workers that two jobs were said to be available for each of the 280,000 who graduated from the universities in 1983. The launching of man-made earth satellites, the mastery of nuclear technology, the synthesis of insulin, as well as innovative research in the fields of agriculture and medicine have already indicated that China has much to contribute to the worldwide scientific community.[26]

Increasing numbers of Chinese scholars and also younger students are going overseas to study. Since 1978 it has been reported that thousands of Chinese students have gone abroad to study; of those, a great number were not state-sponsored. For many such students it is their first opportunity to come in contact with a thoughtful presentation of the Christian faith. Already many have returned to China with a positive attitude toward Christianity because of friends they have made during their overseas stay. Some have entered into a living faith in Christ. Because of their position in society it is very hard for them to make a public Christian confession; many remain secret believers.

Inadequate Health Services

Fifty years ago, there were very few hospitals in rural areas. The city where Ruth and I lived had just one military hospital. At the time of the Revolution, more than half of the hospital beds throughout China were found in Christian institutions. Medical missions had been responsible for introducing Western medicine, and many of the Western-trained doctors were Christians. But most of those hospitals and trained medical personnel were caring for the small proportion of the population living in towns. The vast majority of country people depended entirely on practitioners of traditional medicine who operated shops selling a wide variety of Chinese medicines. Patients with serious illnesses or needing surgery would have to travel 100 miles or more to the nearest mission hospital.

Infant mortality was high. Cholera, typhus and smallpox took the lives of large numbers of people. Surveying the health of the nation in 1949, the new government found hundreds of millions of victims of malaria, schistosomiasis (a disease caused by worms also known as bilharzia or snail fever) and venereal disease. Millions were addicted to opium. Tuberculosis, hookworm and leprosy spread unchecked. Sanitation was lacking almost everywhere and worm infestation was therefore almost universal. Innoculations were almost unknown in the countryside; lice and poverty were equally prevalent.

A marked difference still exists between the city and the countryside in infant mortality (see Fig. 3). Almost one-half of the 3 million medical and health personnel are ministering to the 20 percent of the population now in urban areas.

Nonetheless, great progress in health care has been made. Serious diseases such as cholera, plague, smallpox, typhus and relapsing fevers have been virtually wiped out or at least basically controlled. The number of patients with malaria has dropped from 30 million to 3 million. The average life expectancy has been lengthened from 35 years, before the Revolution, to 68, a truly remarkable improvement—brought about by smaller families, the growing network of rural health centers, as well as the training of a large force of "barefoot doctors" and part-time health workers. Today, former mission hospitals are welcoming medical help from overseas, and even express appreciation to those who founded the institutions and pioneered Western medicine in China.

Although some hospitals lack modern equipment, China has produced medical researchers whose discoveries have

Comparison of Health Statistics 1950–1980[27]

	1950	1980
Mortality rate	25 per 1,000	6.2 per 1,000
Infant mortality	200 per 1,000	12 per 1,000 (urban)
		20-30 per 1,000 (rural)
Life expectancy	Age 35	Age 68
Hospital beds	99,800	2,017,088
Total medical and health personnel	555,040	3,011,038
Qualified medical personnel, including doctors of Western medicine	42,425 41,400	638,549 516,498
Secondary-level medical personnel, including paramedics of Western medicine	118,527 53,400	1,180,665 436,196
Nurses	37,800	474,569
Practitioners of traditional Chinese medicine	286,000	289,502

Figure 3

impressed international medical circles. For example, the American doctors with whom I traveled in 1982 thought highly of work being done in cancer research. The integration of traditional Chinese and Western medicine has been of special interest. The chemical synthesis of insulin by a Chinese research team received worldwide acclaim.

Shortage of Clean Drinking Water

China still faces the problem of providing clean drinking water for large numbers of villages. Government reports indicate that half the population still relies on unsanitary rivers, ponds and shallow wells for drinking water. A loan of $100 million from the World Bank is being used for water improvement projects in eight provinces.

Status of Women

The gospel of Jesus Christ brings liberation to women as well as to men, though often in so-called Christian countries the treatment of women has fallen far short. In the nineteenth century, Christian missionaries in China encouraged education for girls and pioneered adult education for women. They ardently opposed the cruel custom of foot-binding. Early pioneer missionaries also fought against the infanticide of baby girls, a problem still faced by the Chinese government today because of the population problem.

One of the first laws passed by the Communist government was the marriage law of April 1950 abolishing child marriage, polygamy and concubinage.[28] Divorce was made easier, and it was emphasized that husbands and wives are equal before the law and both have divorce and property rights. The divorce rate has increased partly because of the frequent government practice of assigning husband and wife to work in different areas of the country. Article 48 of the new Constitution states:

Women in the People's Republic of China enjoy equal
rights with men in all spheres of life, political, economic, cultural and social, including family life.

The next article declares:

Marriage, the family and mother and child are protected
by the State.[29]

In May 1983 a Chinese government report to the Secretary
General of the United Nations (*The Implementation in the People's Republic of China of the Convention on the Elimination of all
Forms of Discrimination against Women*) emphasized that Chinese women were making full use of their democratic rights of
equality with men and were taking an active part in the political
life of the country. It must be noted, however, that even today
only a few women are found in the higher echelons of government.

Great progress has been made in the education of women
(see Fig. 2), although, as in government, they are less frequently found at higher professional levels.[30] For example, in
Qinghua University in Beijing there were only two females
among the 1984 graduating class of genetic engineers. But one-
third of the nation's scientists and technicians and more than
one-third of the total urban workforce are women.[31]

In the countryside, women still form more than half of the
rural labor force, which means that the majority of them are still
engaged in heavy manual labor. Not infrequently, women can be
seen carrying great loads and hauling heavy carts. Women have
benefited greatly, however, from improved medical services,
and 52 percent of all the workers in medicine and health care are
women. A network of maternity and child-care clinics has cut
down infant mortality and has greatly improved the status of
women's health.

The same government report states:

A powerful nationwide publicity campaign has been
organized to break down the feudal ideas and customs

upholding male superiority. The campaign educates the public about the legal system, especially about the legislation protecting the legitimate rights and interests of women and children, exposes and condemns the discrimination, maltreatment, humiliation, or even persecution of women and children; and motivates the whole society to fight such evil practices.

The Role of Women in the Church

Since the Revolution, women have played an increasingly important role in the Church. In many house churches, pastors were arrested and the work was then carried on by the pastor's wife and other faithful women. Young women have also taken part in evangelistic teams sent out by the house churches. Women are often active in the pastoral committee of the TSPM churches and are sometimes ordained to the ministry.

The testimony of a young woman who serves as an itinerant pastor-evangelist to rural house churches in 10 counties of Henan province was published in 1984. It stated:

I led meetings and pastored the believers. Most meetings were in Christian homes, with numbers ranging from several dozen to several hundred. Very large meetings were held in caverns. As people were busy in the fields during the day, most meetings were held at night. Sometimes they went on until dawn and the Christians wanted to go on! Although the cadres leading the production teams knew about us, they didn't interfere, and some of them were converted . . . .

During the wave of persecution [in 1983], I realized with sorrow that my work was inadequate. In the past I had stressed knowledge and reason, but I had also laid too much stress on miracles and healing. When the persecution came, I saw clearly that my message was "wood, hay, and stubble" and that many believers had not stood the test, but had gone back or even fallen.

But this experience also refined the family of God and it made me deeply aware of the precious reality of Christians praying for each other in times of suffering . . . . Through these fiery trials more fruit is being harvested and even more Christians are engaging in itinerant evangelism and holding meetings. They are also praying more. Five years in the ministry of evangelism have convinced me that God is the only protector and my only support . . . . Even now [mid-1984] many believers and evangelists have not been released.[32]

CRISIS OF FAITH

The Chinese government has always recognized that the new socialist society has spiritual as well as material needs.

> The importance the Chinese leadership gives to the spiritual component is something which constantly surprises other Communists. For the Chinese, dialectical materialism means that spirit and matter are both manifestations of matter itself—indissoluble. As a man thinks, so he acts, and the process of thought and its conditioning have been the subject of intensive study and much debate. The re-making of man, the transformation of motivation, of the spirit's contents, are as essential as the re-making of the Chinese earth; in fact they must be done together. It is in the transformed spirit of the collective that the material strength needed to create a new society finds birth.[1]

The term *spiritual civilization,* which frequently appears in current Chinese Communist literature, is misleading if we are thinking of the Christian view of the spirit. When Chinese Marxists talk about the spiritual needs of society, they are not referring to spirit in the biblical sense. There are two Chinese expressions for "spirit," *jing shen* and *ling hun*. The former is a humanistic term describing mental attitudes and motivation. The latter is a term used for the eternal human spirit. Mao, like Confucius, had nothing to say about eternity; rather he was concerned with creating a *revolutionary* spirit that would motivate people to fulfill his plans for society.

The nationwide network of discussion groups he established, with their emphasis on "Marxism, Leninism, and Mao Zedong Thought," was intended to transform Chinese society from feudal superstition into a Marxist socialist state. Religion was totally rejected. The masses were to be welded together by the force of Mao Zedong Thought alone.

During the Cultural Revolution, the extravagant praise accorded to Mao and the popularity of his famous "little red book," *Quotations from Chairman Mao,* gave him grounds for optimism that his plan was being fulfilled. In 1957 he had stated, "We have won the basic victory in transforming the ownership of the means of production, but we have not yet won complete victory on the political and ideological front."[2] Mao regarded the education of peasantry as of primary importance; he constantly thought of the revolution as being carried out *by* them as well as *for* them. He wrote:

> Apart from their other characteristics, the outstanding thing about China's 600 million people is that they are "poor and blank." This may seem a bad thing, but in reality it is a good thing. Poverty gives rise to the desire for change, the desire for action and the desire for revolution. On a blank sheet of paper free from any mark, the freshest and most beautiful characters can be written, the freshest and most beautiful pictures can be painted.[3]

Mao's great hope rested with the young people.

> You young people, full of vigor and vitality, are in the bloom of life, like the sun at 8 or 9 in the morning. Our hope is placed on you. The world belongs to you. China's future belongs to you.[4]

But in order to keep such a vision alive in the hearts of China's youth, he believed it was necessary to have continuous revolution. These young people were to become the "New Man." They were members of the proletarian class, free from the ideas of the exploiting class. But, according to Mao, only as there was *continual thought reform through labor* would they be able to experience that transformation.

Mao set before the people very high ideals to which everyone was expected to give at least lip service. Yet a great gap existed between the slogans that young people pasted on walls and recited in meetings and their actual practice in daily life.

The Cultural Revolution

Because of that gap, by the end of 1962 Mao was afraid that his revolution might fail and therefore initiated a "socialist education movement." That led to the Cultural Revolution and the frantic attack by the Red Guards on the "Four Olds": old habits, old ideas, old customs, old culture. In it Mao continued to look to the youth of the country to bring about a revival of revolutionary ideology. As has been said, however, instead of setting up a new proletarian order, the "revolutionary masses" divided into factions and attacked each other. Mao's dreams were shattered in the resulting anarchy.

He had not only failed to provide material answers to China's problems, he also was unable to respond to its spiritual needs. Many of these young people, thoroughly disillusioned, escaped and returned illegally to the towns. The visions of glory they had received from Mao in the early days of the Cultural Revolution were now exchanged for harsh reality. They felt betrayed. One young man described his experience in these words, "When I was young, I worshiped Mao."[5] Now the young man's "idol" had fallen and with it, the youth's purpose in life had disappeared. John Fairbank wrote, "Seldom has faith been frustrated on so vast a scale."

Mao recognized that his grandiose schemes had been shipwrecked on the rocks of "self-interest." He had preached "serve the people" and "everything for the public—nothing for one-self," but everywhere people were struggling to preserve their own interests. To many it had seemed that to serve the people really meant to "serve the Party."

Some travelers to China brought reports of the rebirth of the people of China in the image of Mao, a selfless man, dedicated to him and to the service of others. They suggested that the basic characteristics of the Kingdom of God were being revealed in the atheistic society of China. Christians inside China regarded such outside views as naive and deluded.

As a result of Mao's Revolution, people were certainly much more conscious of the needs of the community as a whole. But the individual had not experienced any radical change. The same old evils reappeared in other forms. If Mao could have seen the rejection of his ideals and the disillusionment of youth following his death, he would have felt that the Revolution had been betrayed.

The "New Man"?

Mao had been convinced that the Revolution could be brought about only by people who did not believe in God or in a future life, and therefore had no fear that one day they might face divine judgment. They must have no qualms of conscience that would hinder them from taking violent action against class enemies, those with "bad class status." But once the 1949 Revolution succeeded, Mao found that a new type of person, one who was free from corruption and who was completely dedicated to building a "socialist spiritual civilization" was needed. Marxist theoreticians have always dreamed about a "new man": a person free from corruption, who acted honestly and unselfishly, who freely distributed the "goods that belonged to everyone" and who sought the well-being of the people as a whole. Together with Marx, Mao believed that when economic and social evils were removed from society, there would also be a change for the better in human character.

But what has become increasingly clear is this: The selfishness and corruption of a capitalist society are also present in a socialist society. The belief that human beings are no more than a product of their environment, and that theft, dishonesty and cruelty will disappear if the system is changed, has proven false. The ideology of atheism has not produced the qualities needed to build that new society.

Christians point out that the motivation for an honest and productive society with unselfish service does not spring from Marxist ideology. Christianity has been blamed for hindering violent social change, but when that change does take place, Christians argue that only the new life of Christ can provide the power needed to overcome the self-seeking, dishonesty and corruption so prevalent in modern society. It may well be that a new generation of Chinese leaders will realize the spiritual bankruptcy of Marxism and will be more open to the influence of the gospel of Christ.

The CCP to this day believes that education and modern scientific methods will bring about the new society. It continues to confuse technical ability with moral capacity. Slogans like the "Four Emphases and Five Beautifuls" and campaigns like "Be Courteous Month" all fail to produce people who will always tell the truth and live morally-pure lives. On the crowded buses, pregnant women and the elderly are shown little consideration. As more and more wage and profit incentives are offered, as people see opportunities to get rich, they resort to the old methods of "using the back door"—pulling strings and gaining advantages through friends in influential positions. If one lives in a purely materialistic world, there is always the temptation to use any possible means for personal advantage, regardless of whether or not it is good for society.

So, with the reopening of doors for contact with the world outside China, along with the new possibility of getting rich, came an avalanche of self-seeking. Young people were introduced through radio and TV to space-age comforts and Western gadgets, but saw little chance of significantly improving their own standard of living. The proliferation of ancient evils connected with the "back door" and other forms of corruption led to a wave of crime that was checked only by the drastic steps of the "anti-crime campaign" in 1983. Hundreds of thousands were

arrested and up to 10,000 were executed, most of them young
people 20 to 25 years of age.[6]

A "New Realism" Emerges

In the more relaxed political climate after 1979, the more
educated members of the Mao generation began writing stories
that criticized the excesses of the Cultural Revolution. They
pleaded for liberty to serve humanity instead of politics in their
writing. A "New Realism" literature appeared, emphasizing
humanism and humanitarianism. The characters in its fiction
were not political models to be followed but rather were figures
who appealed to their readers as real people.

> By focusing on the emotions and moods of individ-
> uals, writers of the New Realism also affirmed the
> validity of the inner self—a highly unorthodox notion in
> the Maoist literary tradition.[7]

Quite apart from the dissidents who then became politically
involved, there are also large numbers of young people who
have continued to express their disillusionment and sometimes
their despair about the future. These young people are tired of
politics and struggle. Mao had said that not to have a political
view was to be like a person without a soul. Yet today many
reject the political consciousness that they are supposed to
express in public meetings. They have no faith in high-sounding
phrases that have proved to have little effect on practical daily
life. They have said, "We have heard beautiful words before, and
look where they led"—meaning they led to the Cultural Revolution.

Such alienation between deep personal feelings and outward
expression leads to a sense of unreality and distrust. Many Chinese youth are very cynical, partly because they see little possibility of attaining a system of true justice. With no absolute moral
standards, everything depends on the absolute power of the ruling party; and the average individual does not dare to speak out
against official wrongdoing. Some have given up all hope of any

idealistic solution and instead endeavor only to improve their own living conditions by struggling for some position of personal power.

A modern expression, "hitting the street looking for heat," pictures the restless quest for excitement of China's urban youth, their desire for escape from the dreariness of life and their rebellion against the state's puritanical social code. Sometimes they look for "heat" in underground restaurants and dancing palaces with "pornographic" music from the West. Others, however, who desire meaningful relationships in life and who hunger for love and affection, are much more open to an alternative philosophy—and they may be attracted by Christianity.

Why Is Life's Road Getting Narrower?

In April 1980 *China Youth News* published a letter entitled "Why Is Life's Road Getting Narrower?" The writers were a 23-year-old female factory worker whose parents were Communist Party officials, and a male university student, who represented a panel that had been discussing "Views of Life of Today's Youth." The name *Pan Xiao* was a combination of their two surnames. That letter elicited an unexpected response: 40,000 young people wrote in, echoing the disenchantment expressed by Pan Xiao. Like many of China's youth, Pan Xiao wanted to follow the example of the soldier hero Lei Feng, who had written in a diary found after his death that he wanted to be "a small but useful screw in the machine of socialism." During the Cultural Revolution, however, Pan Xiao witnessed terrible cruelty and violence, contradicting the ideals and slogans "she" had been taught. At the same time there were quarrels within "her" own family and she was betrayed by one of her friends.

As she tried to discover meaning in life, she sought answers from all kinds of people. None of them satisfied her.

> If you say we are here for revolution, the idea is too abstract and far-fetched . . . If you say we live for fame, it is out of reach of the ordinary people . . . If you say we live for mankind, it doesn't match with reality. We

break heads for a few work points, we argue furiously
over the most trivial things . . . If you say we live to
eat, drink and be merry, then we are born naked and
we die as empty shells. But coming into the world for
one go-round seems meaningless, too.[8]

Pan Xiao read countless books but none of them brought satisfaction either. She became convinced that "man is selfish;
there is no such thing as a selfless noble person." The high
ideals taught by Communism seemed ridiculous. She ended by
saying:

Life's road, why is it getting narrower and narrower? I
am already so tired. It is as if I were to let out one more
breath it would mean utter destruction. I confess I have
gone secretly to watch services in the Catholic Church.
I have thought of becoming a nun. I have even thought
of dying . . . My heart is so confused, so contradictory.[9]

The remarkable response to her letter indicates how many
young people share Pan Xiao's disillusionment. She represents
multitudes who started with idealistic views of life, and, inspired
by the revolutionary romanticism of the time, gave all their
strength to the construction of a heaven on earth. From the ear-
liest years in school they had been told that faith in God is a
superstition that has been discarded by modern scientific man:
Bu kao tian ("Do not trust heaven"). Rather, trust in the scientific theories of Marxism they were told.

But then the atrocities of the Cultural Revolution and the
spirit of hatred and distrust that pervaded society made the scientific view of Marxism seem unrealizable. The realities of life
contradicted the earlier theories. "Marxism has crumbled in my
mind," said one student. "The trouble is I do not know how to
get rid of the rubble."[10]

For Pan Xiao, disappointment with family members and
friends in the Party organization came first. During the Cultural
Revolution family members had engaged in mutual criticism and
struggle, resulting in alienation between the generations. Those

experiences cannot be completely forgotten, and even now some subjects cannot be discussed. Second came a sense of the utter selfishness, the lack of any true love, that characterized society. The result was despair. Finally, the very foundations of life were shaken. A "crisis of faith" in Marxism, a realization that all the theories studied in the past led nowhere, brought questions about the true meaning of life.

Longing for Hope

During a time when many young men and women are expressing dissatisfaction with Marxist ideology, Christians have opportunity to point to Christ as the One who alone can satisfy inner emptiness. The enthusiasm and romanticism of the early days of the Revolution have evaporated. The atheist and materialist ideology has failed to produce the noble man capable of promoting the socialist spiritual civilization to which Deng Xiaoping referred in 1982 at the Party's 12th National Congress, and then again in 1984.[11]

If ideology makes the man, Christians can point to the ideology of the One who lived an absolutely righteous life and offered up His life on the cross in order to bring reconciliation and forgiveness to men and women of all nations. It was through His love and the power of His resurrection that the early disciples were able to put His teaching into practice.

In the first Christian community the rich sold their goods and made the money available to meet the needs of the poor. Dishonesty, cheating and lying were condemned in the early church. Whether it is the selfish individualism in a capitalist society or the spiritual bankruptcy and corruption of the Marxist system, all come under the judgment of Christ. The troubled young people in China's present-day society need to meet Christians who will show love and understanding and demonstrate the power of Christ in dealing with life's problems.

It is not easy to bring about a meeting of Christian and non-Christian minds in China. The government is extremely sensitive to any attempts to introduce Christianity to students. Further, many Christians find it difficult to explain their faith in ways that answer the questions of young people brought up in the Marxist society. The rapid growth in the number of young people who have become Christians in recent years, however, points to the fact that many who have been in trouble have come to realize that Christ does offer hope, both for this life and for the life to come.

A longing for hope comes through in some of the stories being written by China's young authors. In the story "Love Cannot Be Forgotten," for example, author Zhang Jie records the last words taken from his mother's diary:

> I am a person who believes in materialism. Yet now I am eagerly waiting for heaven. If there is truly a so-called heaven I know you must be waiting there for me. I am going there soon to meet you and we shall be together forever. Never again will we have to fear affecting another person's life and so separate ourselves. Dear, wait for me. I am coming.[12]

With those words the writer depicted the sadness of unfulfilled love and also a yearning focused on the possibility of a future life.

Spiritual Pollution

Where can China's youth find love in society and hope for the future? Christians would naturally point to the love of God in Christ. But the government is determined to keep out all forms of spiritual "pollution"—which it identifies with any influence thought to be detrimental to the development of socialist society.[13] There is no longer the extreme emphasis on ideology that characterized the Cultural Revolution. On the other hand, young people are still required to maintain a materialist view of life. Modernization calls for emphasis on science and technology. The only truth is said to be that which can be scientifically proven, and therefore modern youth must accept a materialistic view of the universe and the creation of life.

This policy was evident in the Anti-Spiritual Pollution Movement,[14] launched in autumn 1983. Party members were urged to fight against "acts of spiritual pollution." Four categories of spiritual pollution were listed as: spreading obscenities or reactionary statements; vulgar taste in performances; efforts to seek personal gain, or indulgence in individualism, anarchism or liberalism; writing or saying things counter to the country's social system as laid out in the Constitution.

At first it seemed that the movement would lead to further restrictions on writers, who were urged not to be too humanistic or too concerned with self-expression. Once again, because of warnings about the danger of undesirable decadent influences from the West, many were afraid of having contacts with foreigners. People were even fearful that the campaign might indicate a return to some of the "leftist" policies of the past, and would lead to another reign of terror. Deng Xiaoping, however, put a stop to the movement when it appeared that it might get out of hand. What if it hindered relations with people from the West, and thus affected China's progress in the Four Modernizations program?

By early December 1983 there was an easing of the pressure. It was decided that the Anti-Spiritual Pollution Movement should not be taken to the countryside, where 80 percent of the people live.

Further, it was stated that "spiritual pollution must be clearly separated from legitimate religions." When Archbishop Robert Runcie from England asked China's president whether the campaign was aimed against religious people, he was told very definitely that it had nothing to do with religion. But during the movement's early months, opposition had increased toward those who would not work within the TSPM, even if not as a direct result.[15] There were reports of at least 200 Christians being arrested in Henan; other provinces were also affected.

It is true that China's increasing contacts with the outside world have opened doors for all kinds of undesirable elements from the West. Christian English teachers in China are often embarrassed when they see their non-Christian compatriots introducing a life-style, literature and music they feel can only be harmful. It is not easy for them to explain that Western nations are far from being Christian and that much that characterizes

Western culture is in opposition to the Kingdom of God. Christians can, however, demonstrate through their own lives the difference between Christian and non-Christian behavior. Certainly the Church in China supports the government in opposition to the spiritual pollution of Western culture's "evil" influences.

On the other hand, along with the determination to keep out pornographic and other undesirable materials, the government also opposes the entrance of all religious literature. In one case, the Bible was displayed alongside pornographic magazines as contraband materials. While the Bible is not an illegal book if printed in China, the government is clearly opposed to the widespread distribution of Christian literature. From the Marxist viewpoint the message of Christ is a spiritual pollutant. Although it does not cause Christians to oppose the government and its Four Modernization policies, it produces a different world view and thus undermines basic Marxist philosophy.

The Chinese government, therefore, has to think of ways of allowing a measure of religious freedom while at the same time doing everything possible to prevent young people from being influenced by the gospel of Christ. Criticizing people's tendency to turn to religion, *China Youth News* magazine stated:

> The Party should provide the solution [to any of life's problems] through warmth and understanding—only then shall youth no longer turn to other worldly beings for assistance.[16]

Often local officials will attempt to launch campaigns against those who openly confess their faith in Christ and encourage other young people to believe. This is shown in a letter from a Christian written at the end of 1983:

> Recently, the anti-spiritual pollution campaign was started in our city and some of our young believers are meeting very strong pressure because they had openly admitted they were Christians.
>
> Previously they had encouraged their workmates and fellow-students to go to church. But now the lead-

ers in their units are seeking them out to talk to them, and consider that they have serious spiritual pollution because they not only believe in Christianity themselves but urge others to believe and go to worship, thus being intermediaries for spiritual pollution.

One girl was sought out by the leaders several times and was very nervous. She didn't know how to reply, as she had never experienced this kind of spiritual and mental pressure.

Her friends who had gone with her to hear the gospel preached have already written guarantees for their work-unit that they will not believe, and have urged her to keep her faith to herself and not express it. But at home the older people have told her to be strong.

Another girl . . . has been questioned several times and my own niece . . . has had the same trouble.

None of them have been through the fierce struggles of the Cultural Revolution, and until now have not met with difficulties. So they don't know what to do to meet this new situation.

At present the spearhead of the anti-spiritual pollution campaign is aimed at young people, and apparently will last a long time. Young Christians are afraid they will not be able to endure. Please will you and your colleagues pray urgently for our young brothers and sisters . . . [17]

The same kind of pressure from the government was referred to by a Christian student who wrote describing attempts made by his teacher to bring about a change in his faith.

Our school has introduced a new lesson called "Materialism." Although the lecturer is very kind and helps us with many indoor and outdoor activities, I won't give up my faith for her. It would be very difficult not to believe the principal of materialism if I had not listened to the gospel broadcasts and my Christian friends.

The truth of Christianity has been distorted. In my

history class, Jesus Christ is just a man. In the political class the Creator becomes a playboy, and jeering prevails in the classroom. These pressures make it difficult for me. I am made fun of, but I pray that God will give me power and courage and keep me close to Him. I pray for my unbelieving relatives and friends.[18]

Power for Life

Christians in China must show understanding and be able to answer the questions that disillusioned youth are asking: "What is the nature of man?" "What is the meaning of life?" "Does the individual have a real value or is he or she only a screw in the machinery of the revolution?" "There is much discussion about justice, but how can standards of justice be maintained without absolute values?"

When the students first hear the gospel, they are faced with a multitude of questions resulting from their Marxist education. One final-year medical student who began to read the Bible started at Genesis 1:1 and noted that this verse assumed the existence of God. She asked:

> How do I know there is a God? Marxist-Leninist Thought teaches that Darwin's theory of evolution is fact and that there is no Creator God. It [Marxist-Leninist Thought] also teaches that man is good and is getting better and that Jesus Christ was just an ordinary man.[19]

Two weeks later the same student, after reading the Gospels, observed, "I see now that I need to have faith before I can solve my problems relating to Marxist-Leninist Thought." She shares the fact today that faith has come to her with power and conviction.

Even though Confucius (Chinese philosopher, 551-479 B.C.) was attacked during the Cultural Revolution, people are still much influenced by Confucian ethics; the anti-Confucian campaign is seen to have been a mistake. But Confucian ethics are based on relationships—social integration with family, neighbor and state—which were so seriously damaged during the Cultural Revolution. Wounds inflicted at that time are not easily healed; the atmosphere of mistrust is not easily dispelled. People who attacked one another during those disastrous years of struggle are now working together again, but they need a spirit of love to bring true reconciliation.

Christians in China today have opportunity to show that in Christian faith there is a solution to many of these problems. It is not enough to repeat gospel ideals. The Chinese people have listened to all kinds of high-sounding principles, but now they must see that in belief in Christ there is power to put into practice the ethical teaching of the Kingdom of God.

Some time ago a Chinese professor in America, who had just become a Christian, compared some of the teaching of Confucius with parts of the Sermon on the Mount. He said, "The important thing about Christianity is that it has power. We have had good ethical teaching for thousands of years, but we have not had the power to put it into effect. For this reason the resurrection of Jesus Christ is so very important."

Message of New Life Offers Hope

It is this message of new life—forgiveness, reconciliation, and hope through the death and resurrection of Christ—that has meaning for young people in China today. As they see many Christians obviously possessing peace and joy and demonstrating love in their relationships, together with uncompromising refusal to be involved in dishonest practices, they are drawn to the Saviour of the world. This is what one listener to a Christian radio station wrote:

> Ever since I started school, I was brought up under atheism and had no concept of religious belief. In the past, I thought that believing in God was superstitious, feudalistic, and that man had created a god rather than God created man.

However, by a very unexpected chance, my viewpoint was completely changed. In an evening last summer when I was lying down listening to the radio, twiddling the knob unintentionally, I suddenly heard a voice proclaiming "because He is God . . ." I only listened to your broadcast once in a while just to dispel my boredom and to entertain myself. But I never regarded your message as truth.

However, I began to doubt the view I had held hitherto. Is there really a God? Is the world created by God or by men? These questions wheeled around in my mind many times a day. Over and over I denied that there was a God, only to affirm my atheism. But every time I listened to your program, my faith in atheism collapsed . . .

Following those periods of frustration, I constantly listened to your programs and now I have become a Christian and believe in God. The process of conversion from an atheist to a Christian (I don't know if I can be thus called) is not a simple matter and it is difficult to put into words.

A "socialist spiritual civilization" without God leaves vast numbers of people dissatisfied. Only a few of the letters they write reach any Christian radio station. The first letter the Far East Broadcasting Company received from one writer in China was the thirty-sixth he had written, and he was complaining that he had received no answer. Enough letters do arrive, however, to show that many are seeking answers to questions about the origin of the universe and the purpose of human existence. God has not left Himself without a witness.

The Word of God comes not only over the radio waves, but also through the lives of Christians. Those who become Christians bear witness that frustration and despair are replaced by the reconciling love of Christ and the peace that comes through the indwelling Spirit of God.

GOVERNMENT RELIGIOUS POLICY

Chinese society abounds in contradictions, or *maodun* (see Glossary). The antireligious Marxist theory expressed in government documents sometimes seems far removed from the warm reception given foreign Christian visitors by high officials. Such visitors are assured that the policy of religious freedom is being fully implemented. Chinese religious leaders report on the government's helpfulness in Church affairs.

But Christians living in China, with many years' experience of frustrations, restrictions and sometimes direct persecution, often tell a different story. Western visitors, who are usually limited to official contacts, rarely have opportunity to hear those firsthand accounts.

Differing Viewpoints

Descriptions of freedom of religion prepared for the international news media are sometimes very different from the internal communications intended for government cadres. However free and relaxed they may appear, spokesmen at TSPM-controlled churches usually keep carefully within the bounds laid down by the CCP. Even among CCP members, however, there may be different viewpoints. Some render lip service to ideological theories, but are much more pragmatic in their attitude. Others, whatever impression they give to visitors, are fully committed to Marxist policies.

In order to understand present religious trends in China, therefore, we must consider not only the public announcements, but also the internal statements of policy which are studied and implemented by CCP members. Policies may not be fully or consistently implemented, but they do show the direction in which the government is moving. At the same time, we must never forget that the hearts of "kings" are in the Lord's hands (see Prov. 21:1). Further, there may well be a change in the attitude of the younger leaders who will succeed the present generation.

The Scriptures give us clear examples of rulers (like Cyrus), who were raised up to fulfill God's purpose. Our attitude therefore must always be one of faith as we intercede for government leaders, believing that God is able to overrule and change even Communist policies. At the same time, like many Chinese Christians, we must realize that God may allow further suffering to come to His faithful servants. Chinese Christians, conscious of the spiritual conflict, are especially aware of the basic principles lying behind government religious policy.

Long-term goals and short-term strategies must be clearly distinguished if we are to understand the CCP attitude to Christianity. That attitude is grounded in classical Marxist materialist dogma, buttressed by nineteenth-century scientific thought. Marxism-Leninism asserts that religion belongs to humanity's backward ages and cannot be allowed to hold back evolutionary progress.

Marxism and Christianity are mutually-exclusive world views. Marxism is fundamentally atheistic, based on the assumption that matter is all there is. Man has no spirit, nor is there life after death. Mao's genius was his ability to take a Western system of thought and adapt it to Chinese culture; Marxism-Leninism was thus metamorphosed into something uniquely Chinese. Nevertheless, in matters of religion, Mao conformed to basic Communist doctrine.

The China of Chairman Mao was to be the "kingdom of man." "Our god is none other than the masses of the Chinese people."[1] After the 1949 Revolution, Ruth and I used to hear the children singing, *Bu bai tian, Bu bai di, Jiu yao bai renmin laodong li* (Don't worship heaven, don't worship earth, only worship the labor of the masses). Mao Zedong's statement in 1940 still represents the basic CCP viewpoint:

> Communists may form an anti-imperialist and anti-feudal united front for political action with certain idealists and even with religious followers, but we can never approve of their idealism or religious doctrines.[2]

Although Deng Xiaoping's economic reforms have been completely contrary to Mao's policies during the last years of his life, his basic ideology is still Communist. In a speech published in March 1985 he said, "We should not allow young people to become captives of capitalist ideologies or ideals . . . We must let our people, including our children, know that we are sticking to socialism and Communism." The ultimate goal of China's modernization is to build a Communist society.

That same attitude was seen in a statement by an official of the Religious Affairs Bureau (RAB) to a TSPM gathering in Beijing in September 1982:

> Respect for and protection of freedom of religious belief is our Party's basic policy on religious questions. This is a long-term policy and should be consistently implemented until the future time when religion naturally disappears.[3]

Thus, in the light of long-term Marxist thinking, the policy of religious liberty is seen as a strategy for the present, not in conflict with the ultimate goal of a society in which religion will cease to exist. The government of China has not changed its view that religion is a harmful "opiate" of the people, and that real leadership of the country itself must be in the hands of atheistic Marxists.

It would be helpful to view chronologically how these fundamental policies have actually been implemented over the last

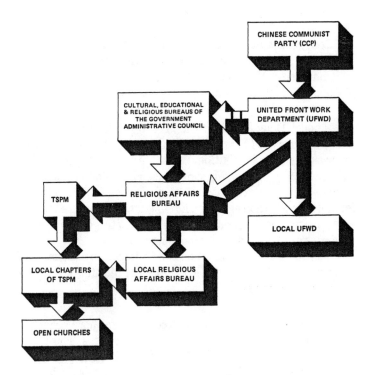

TSPM AND THE GOVERNMENT

three decades. The various periods may be summarized as follows:

1. 1949-1966: Increasing totalitarian control, pressure and persecution of the Church.

2. 1966-1976: The Cultural Revolution—total suppression of religion by extreme leftists.

3. 1977-present: Reinstitution of more moderate policies; opening to the West.

Increasing Control, Pressure and Persecution of the Church

During the 1949-1966 period a limited amount of freedom was granted but with increasing pressures being placed on the Church. In 1950, the "Christian Manifesto,"[4] essentially drawn up under the direction of Premier Zhou Enlai, was signed by a majority of Protestant leaders and by many Christians throughout the country. It served to rid the Church of foreign influences and ties, and thus prepared the way for the preparatory committee of the TSPM to be formed the following year.

It is important to see clearly the origin of the TSPM and its place in the overall system of control used by the government (see chart: TSPM and the Government). The arm of government for supervising various non-Communist sectors in the new society is the United Front Work Department (UFWD).[5]

The United Front policy was perfected by the CCP in its struggles both with the Nationalists led by Chiang Kai-shek and with the Japanese. It involves winning over the majority of sectors of society to support or at least acquiesce in its policies, while reducing to an ineffective minority, isolating, neutralizing and ultimately destroying die-hard opposition. The UFWD was charged with obtaining the cooperation of such diverse groups as the national minorities (e.g., non-Han peoples in the southwest), rich peasants, national bourgeoisie (businessmen and industrialists) and members of the various religions. In the period of transition from a so-called semi-colonial, semi-feudal society to a socialist state, the contributions of these nonrevolutionary elements could nonetheless be used for revolutionary ends.

From 1949 onward, the minimum conditions for participation in the United Front were anti-imperialism and patriotism, defined as love for socialism and the New China under the leadership of the CCP.

Since the rise to power of Deng Xiaoping in 1978, a further factor was added, perhaps now the most important: A willingness to support the Party's Four Modernizations program of socialist construction. The UFWD controls and staffs the RAB which in turn controls the "patriotic" religious organizations, including the TSPM and the China Christian Council (see Note 19).

An article in the Party's ideological magazine, *Red Flag,* describes the functions of these organizations as: (1) Helping the Party and the state implement the policy of freedom of religious belief, (2) helping the religious leaders and followers to heighten their patriotic and socialist consciousness, and (3) organizing and leading the religious masses in engaging in normal religious activities.

The TSPM is responsible to the RAB and serves as a liaison between the government and the churches. It should be noted that the TSPM is not a church in itself; rather all relationships between churches and state have to be channeled through it. As a national administrative office it controls all the churches that have been allowed to open and function in the prescribed manner. Article 29 of its constitution makes explicit the mingling of political and religious aims in the TSPM:

This committee is the anti-imperialist, patriotic association of Chinese Christians and it has the following objectives: Under the leadership of the Chinese Communist Party and the People's Government, it shall unite all Christians in China, to foster the love for our country, to respect the law of the land, to hold fast to the principles of self- government, self-support and self-propagation, and that of the church's independence and self-determination, to safeguard the achievements of the Three-Self Patriotic Movement, to assist the government in implementing the policy of religious freedom, to contribute positively toward building up a modernized and strong socialistic China with a high degree of democracy and a highly developed civilization, toward the return of Taiwan to the motherland and the realization of national unity, toward opposition to hegemonism and the maintenance of world peace.

During the early 1950s the CCP gradually clamped down on all existing independent religious bodies and brought them under TSPM control. Church members had to attend political training classes in the churches, and were ordered not only to criticize themselves, but others too, at special self-criticism meetings. One prominent TSPM leader, Liu Liangmo, secretary of the YMCA, wrote an article on "How to Hold a Successful Accusation Meeting." It stated:

One of the central tasks at present for Christian churches and groups across the nation is to hold successful accusation meetings. Big accusation meetings constitute a most effective means of helping the masses of believers to comprehend the evil wrought in China by imperialism, to recognize the fact that imperialism has utilized Christianity to attack China, and to wipe out imperialist influences within the church.[6]

He justified criticism meetings in the churches by saying that "Jesus' reprimands to the scribes and Pharisees of that time were certainly accusations." That the whole process was being manipulated by the CCP is made clear by a further statement in that article:

Throughout the whole process of preparation for the big accusation meeting, we ought to invite the RAB of the local people's government or other related offices, democratic political groups and other concerned parties to come and advise. The texts of outstanding accusations ought to be recorded and given to local papers for publishing. Also mailed to the preparation committee of the Chinese Christian Oppose America Assist Korea Three-Self Reform Movement Committee.

Accusation meetings made it impossible to maintain a spirit of love and obedience to the truth within the churches. As Christians attacked one another, the Spirit of the Lord was grieved. Many sought to avoid the institutional church altogether. Thus, the beginnings of the house-church movement can be traced back to such developments in the early '50s.

Many pastors who refused to cooperate with the TSPM in this way were eventually arrested and jailed, often for many years. The most outstanding example was Wang Mingdao, who was arrested in August 1955 after the TSPM had whipped up a nationwide "Accuse Wang Mingdao" campaign. Many other pastors and evangelists who refused to take part in TSPM political activities were branded as counterrevolutionaries, and were imprisoned. In April 1984, Bishop Ding Guangxun, present leader of the TSPM, told Hong Kong reporters that the only period during which the Church had suffered was that of the Cultural Revolution (1966 to 1976).[7] Such a statement ignores the fact that hundreds of Christian pastors and church workers were arrested during the 1950s and spent years in prison before the Cultural Revolution. Many of them have been rehabilitated and released only since 1979.

Also during that earlier period, the number of churches was drastically reduced by the TSPM under the pretext of doing away with denominations. Most rural churches had already been closed in 1950-1953 during the Land Reform campaign.[8] But pressures were eventually brought to bear in the cities too. A document of the TSPM Committee in the northern city of Taiyuan, capital of Shanxi province, described the Church reorganization there after local pastors had undergone socialist education and professed Party loyalty (See Appendix 1). Unified worship was set up in one church for the whole city, to be led by a ministerial staff of three or four. All administration of church affairs came under the control of the TSPM committee. Hymns would be "edited." Further,

> The books used to interpret the Bible in every church will be examined, criticized, and those containing poison will be rejected. Only teaching favoring unity and socialism will be promoted.[9]

Preaching too was to be controlled, with such subjects as the Last Days, "vanity" and "the difference between belief and unbelief in marriage" forbidden.

A similar report from Wenzhou, in recent years a thriving center of house-church activities, stated:

> From its beginnings the church in Wenzhou has been a tool to enslave and carry out aggression against the Chinese people in the Zhejiang region . . . The Methodists were controlled by British imperialism, and the Seventh-Day Adventists and the China Inland Mission by American imperialism . . . After discussion everyone felt that the most important advantages in uniting the churches were: to thoroughly smash the plots of imperialism to divide and rule; to eradicate illegal happenings within the church; and for financial affairs to be united so that personnel and property were used to their best advantage, and that which is left over can go to support socialist construction.[10]

It is not surprising that, under strict control, church attendance decreased, and churches ceased to exercise an effective Christian witness. By late 1958, only four churches were left open in Beijing where previously there had been 64; in Shanghai 200 churches were reduced to 23; and in other centers the number was reduced to between one and four.[11]

On the eve of the Cultural Revolution, therefore, the TSPM had already reduced the institutional church to a shadow of its former self.

The Cultural Revolution—
Total Suppression of Religion

As has been said, the decade of 1966-1976 marked the Cultural Revolution. During the early '60s, Party theoreticians had debated on how to deal with religion.[12] The more moderate wanted to make a clear distinction between legitimate religious activities and superstition, arguing that purely ideological means, not coercion, should be used to convince religious believers of their errors. In contrast, those further to the left believed that "peaceful coexistence" between the Party and religious elements was impossible, and that religion had always been an opiate. "Class struggle" the leftists said should be carried out not merely against superstitious beliefs such as fortune telling, but also against the religious beliefs of Catholics, Protestants, Buddhists and Muslims.

In 1965, the leftist hard-liners triumphed. Persecution during the Cultural Revolution was a natural outgrowth of the belief that religion must be destroyed by force. Among the "Four Olds," which the Red Guards were commissioned to destroy, was religion. Religious buildings were desecrated and all were closed down. Religious symbols and literature were banned. Any expression of religious beliefs, even the wearing of a cross, resulted in persecution. A Red Guard wall poster, pasted on a former YMCA building in August 1966, stated:

> There is no God; there is no spirit; there is no Jesus
> . . . how can adults believe in these things? . . . Like
> Islam and Catholicism, Protestantism is a reactionary
> feudal ideology, the opium of the people, with foreign
> origins and contacts . . . We are atheists; we believe
> only in Mao Zedong. We call on all people to burn
> Bibles, destroy images and disperse religious associa-
> tions.[13]

During that terrible period, Christians had their homes ransacked, and their Bibles and other books confiscated or burned.

Many were imprisoned or sent to do forced labor. Some were cruelly tortured, and some under such agonizing pressures were driven to suicide.[14]

We now know that, even during the Cultural Revolution, Christians in some areas continued to meet secretly for fellowship. Many more kept the faith in their hearts, without any outward practice. A former fellow worker described how during the worst period his Bible had been hidden away by a friend. Later, when he was able to retrieve it, his wife divided it up into small portions and sewed them together so that they could be used separately. In that way, if he was found reading the Scriptures, he would lose only one section of his Bible.

Reinstitution of More Moderate Policies

The period from 1977 to the present has had both encouraging and discouraging aspects. During the tragic years of the Cultural Revolution, it seemed to many observers that the leftists' goal of destroying the power of religion had been achieved. Today, however, the government recognizes that persecution failed to overcome the faith of millions of Chinese Christians. The suffering through which Christians passed is now blamed on the Cultural Revolution, epitomized by the Gang of Four who dominated the scene during the last years of Mao Zedong's life.

Following Mao's death on September 9, 1976, and the subsequent overthrow of the radical Gang of Four in October of that year, pressures on the Church eased somewhat. But it was not until Deng Xiaoping had firmly grasped the reins of power in 1978, inaugurating the dramatically new policy of modernization and more openness to the West, that the government began seriously to reconsider its policy toward religion.

In early 1977 the RAB, which had been closed by the extremists during the Cultural Revolution, was allowed by the CCP to resume work. In the same year several "patriotic" religious figures, including Bishop Ding, reappeared at official government functions for the first time in many years. Sixteen such figures, representing their various religions, took part in a meeting of the Chinese People's Political Consultative Conference in

March 1978. The various patriotic religious associations were being resurrected behind the scenes.

Gradually it became clear that the CCP and the government had decided to reinstate the religious structures of the 1950s and were allowing, once again, a limited degree of religious toleration. In spring 1979, the first few churches were reopened under the auspices of the TSPM. The "show" church in Beijing, which had been permitted to exist for foreign diplomats and foreign visitors since the early '70s, was now allowed to readmit Chinese.

Christians took full advantage of Deng Xiaoping's "liberal" period (i.e., the "Beijing Spring," roughly 1979-1981), when political controls were eased and the CCP allowed a greater degree of free speech at the Democracy Wall in Beijing. In various cities the few reopened churches were packed with people, many of them young. In both city and countryside the house churches made rapid gains, seizing the opportunity to evangelize and to hold large meetings.

In that great turnaround from Cultural Revolution policies, Party officials feared to be accused of being "leftist" and often turned a blind eye to Christian activities.[15] As a result it soon became evident that China was experiencing something of a religious revival. In the ideological vacuum left by the virtual collapse of Maoism as a pseudo-religion, many people were turning to religion. Superstitious practices revived, particularly in the countryside, but many found the Christian faith appealing. Temples and mosques were also opened.

The CCP was faced with the undeniable fact that, far from withering away, Christianity had multiplied in strength and was flourishing. The pressing problem for the government was how to bring this movement under control and ultimately limit its influence, particularly among young people. The government was thus faced with three problems: (1) how to explain the great increase of Christians, (2) how to explain the turnabout in religious policy to confirmed Marxist cadres who were expecting to continue harsh treatment of religionists, and (3) how actually to carry out the new policy.

The first is a problem because the church was supposed to have greatly shrunk, if not to have disappeared altogether, after a generation of socialist influence. The fact that the reverse has happened is a source of no little concern. Articles in the Chinese press have sought to answer such questions as, "Why do Communists, who are atheists, advocate freedom of religious belief? Is this policy sincere or is it simply expedient? What is meant by freedom of religion?"

By 1982 the Party and government had assessed the situation and promulgated two important documents. The first was *Document 19*, a major circular outlining religious policy, issued by the Central Committee of the CCP. The second was the revised National Constitution.

Document 19 of the CCP Central Committee

The full title of the circular known as *Document 19* is: "Concerning Our Country's Basic Standpoint and Policy on Religious Questions During the Socialist Period." This document, sent confidentially to Party committees across the country at the end of March 1982, lays down definitive guidelines for the control and supervision of religious believers in China. Since it emanates from the highest Party echelons, all other public statements need to be seen in its light.

(a) Marxist Ideology and Religion

The main body of *Document 19* opens by describing present CCP attitudes toward religion:

> Religion is a historical phenomenon of a certain stage in the development of human society. It has its stages of growth, development and disappearance . . . After the rise of a class society the most profound social factors that gave rise to religion, enabling it to survive and develop were the control by these blind social, alien forces from which the people could not free themselves; in the despair and fear of the laborers under the great suffering caused by the system of exploitation;

and in the need of the exploiting class to use religion as
a narcotic and as an important spiritual means to control
the masses.

Thus it is clear from the outset that, however liberal present
Party policy may appear in its implementation compared to the
horrors of the Cultural Revolution, it is still based on the old,
rigid Marxist assumptions.[16] The document continues:

In a socialist society, along with the elimination of the
system of exploitation and the elimination of the exploiting class, the class factor that has given rise to the existence of religion has already been basically eliminated.[17]

In other words, religion, in principle, has no place in a socialist
society such as the People's Republic of China. It is only a relic
left over by the old society.

However, whereas the Gang of Four and other leftist zealots
believed that religion could be eradicated immediately by force,
China's present rulers take a more realistic and lenient view:

In human history, religion will ultimately disappear, but
it will only naturally disappear after a long period of
development of socialism and communism, after all the
objective conditions have been fulfilled.

They accept, at least in theory, that the use of force is unrealistic and counterproductive:

All the comrades in our Party should adequately and
soberly understand the long-term nature of religious
questions under socialist conditions. It is unrealistic to
think that religion will soon wither away after the socialist system has been established and the economy and
culture have developed to a certain degree. The idea
and practice that treats religion as something we can
eliminate once and for all by administrative orders or
even by the means of force, even more runs counter to

the basic Marxist viewpoint on religious questions and is completely wrong and extremely harmful.

They realize that the erroneous policies of the Cultural Revolution period not only alienated the religious populace but, as was feared by the more perceptive Marxists, served to multiply the attraction of religious faith:

> After 1959, "Leftist" mistakes in our religious work gradually began to develop and by the middle of the sixties became even more serious . . . [The Leftists] used violence to solve religious problems so that religious activities even had some development in a situation where they were dispersed and in secret.

The decision to shun violence is to be heartily applauded. But the arrest of many Protestant and Roman Catholic believers at the end of 1983 shows that the Party is still not adverse to bending its own rules in situations the Party deems necessary. However, the fact that, at the highest level of the Party, outright persecution on the massive scale perpetrated during the Cultural Revolution is now condemned, has undoubtedly led to an improved situation for religious believers.

(b) CCP Control of Religion: The United Front

In China, it is unthinkable that religion should be allowed freedom to develop without Party control. The Party seeks to control every facet of life, and religion is no exception—the more so since it is viewed as an ideological force hostile to Marxism. *Document 19* states unequivocally:

> Strengthening Party leadership is the basic guarantee for dealing properly with religious questions. The Party's religious work is an important component part of the Party's "United Front" work and mass work and involves many aspects of social life.

As we have seen, the UFWD, which is directly responsible to the Central Committee of the CCP, controls the whole array of "people's organizations," including the TSPM. Bishop Ding has stated that the TSPM and the China Christian Council are *not* controlled by the State. *Document 19*, however, says:

> Our Party committees at all levels must powerfully direct and organize all relevant departments, including the United Front departments; the Religious Affairs Bureaus; the Minorities Affairs departments; the Legal departments; the Propaganda, Culture, Scientific and Health departments; and the Trades Unions; the Communist Youth League; the Women's Federation and other people's organizations, to unify their thinking, understanding and policies, and to share the work responsibility, cooperating closely to resolutely take this important task in hand [i.e., religious work].

Although nominally independent as "people's organizations," the TSPM and other "patriotic" religious bodies, in fact, operate under Party supervision and play a vital role in insuring Party control over religious believers.

The RAB would also deny that it interferes at all with teaching given by the Church, but here we read that Party-controlled branches are ordered to "powerfully direct and organize" religious groups with a view to influencing their thinking. It goes without saying, therefore, that the TSPM must conduct church activities in accordance with Party guidelines.

(c) CCP Control: Patriotic Religious Organizations

The government recognizes eight national patriotic religious organizations five of which are Christian (Protestant and Catholic).[18] The CCP defines the role of these organizations as follows:

> The *basic task* of the patriotic religious organizations *at all levels* is to assist the government in carrying out the policy of freedom of religious beliefs and the person-

alities of the religious circles continuously to raise their patriotic and socialist awareness, to represent the legitimate rights and interests of religious believers, to organize and lead the masses of religious believers to carry out normal religious activities and satisfactorily to do all the work related to religion. All the patriotic religious organizations should obey the leadership of the Party and the government (italics ours).

The document gives the figure of 3,400 or more professional Catholic religious workers and 5,900 or so Protestant pastoral workers. It states laconically: "Through many years of natural elimination the present number of professional religious workers is much less than at liberation." The official attitude toward them is:

We must unite them, show concern for them and help them to *progress*. We must steadfastly and patiently teach them to *love our country*, observe the law and support socialism, the cause of the reunification of the motherland and national unity. Among Catholics and Protestants we should intensify education in *maintaining independence* and running the church on their own (italics ours).

Since this is a statement by an avowedly atheistic bureaucracy, "progress" does not connote spiritual growth. Certainly it does not mean what Paul meant when he set forth the goals of the Spirit for the church:

Admonishing every man and teaching every man with all wisdom, that we may present every man complete in Christ . . . until we all attain to the unity of the faith, and of the knowledge of the Son of God, to a mature man, to the measure of the stature which belongs to the fulness of Christ (see Col. 1:28, Eph. 4:13).

Rather, *Document 19* means progress along socialist lines.

It is also noteworthy that "love of country" is the goal always mentioned first—just as in the title of the Three-Self *Patriotic* Movement, the emphasis is on patriotism. "Maintaining independence" means independence from the Vatican or other foreign church bodies, but not from the CCP. Christ, on the other hand, prayed for a Church united in keeping His word, sanctified in the truth and dependent on His sustaining power (See John 17).

(d) Training of Patriotic Religious Leaders

Many of the present leaders in the patriotic religious associations are elderly. The Party sees the need, therefore, for "systematic training and education of a young generation of patriotic religious workers." Several theological seminaries have been reopened in China, the most famous of which is Nanjing Theological Seminary, now frequently visited by overseas religious leaders and delegations. According to *Document 19*:

> The task of the religious colleges is to train a rank of young professional religious workers who politically love the motherland, support the Party's leadership and the socialist system, and who are to a certain extent accomplished in religious learning.

This statement explains the importance of political instruction in the TSPM seminaries. These young religious workers are to become "under Party leadership, a strong core guaranteeing that our religious organizations maintain their activities in the right direction."

In light of all that, it seems almost superfluous to add that "the right direction" is decided by whatever may be the Party's current political line.

(e) Religious Policy and International Relations

The CCP is very aware of the important role religion plays in international affairs, recognizing that "the external contacts of our religious circles . . . play an important role in expanding our country's political influence."

We in the Church outside China should not therefore naively ignore the political dimensions of the many visits made abroad by TSPM leadership in recent years. The CCP also gives a warning against:

> . . . reactionary religious forces in the world, especially the Roman Curia and Protestant missions [who] are also attempting to exploit every opportunity to carry out infiltrating activities in order to "stage a return to China." Our policy is resolutely to resist the infiltration of any hostile foreign forces as well as to vigorously develop international friendly exchanges in the religious field.

That outlook explains the recent visits of various TSPM delegations to Europe, North America, Australia, New Zealand and Africa.

Outside organizations that will completely support TSPM policy and will refrain from giving assistance to those who are not satisfied with its limitations both on evangelism and on independent teaching ministries are to be welcomed. Any who seek to reach China through radio, literature or in other ways are to be resolutely opposed. A recent statement on this question comes from Yang Jingren, head of the UFWD, who spoke at a 1984 celebration marking TSPM's thirtieth anniversary. He said:

> In recent years certain hostile foreign forces have used China's open-door policy . . . to smuggle large quantities of religious publications into the hinterland of China, and carried out "Gospel broadcasting," regarding China as a "new mission field" and vainly hoping to "stage a return to China." Some people have sent others to infiltrate China to collect information, and set up secret organizations, and carry out subversive activities.[19]

Yang emphasized that "This is absolutely forbidden. They must never . . . distribute [such publications]."

(f) Controlling Growth and the House Churches

In *Document 19* the CCP refers specifically to Christian house churches.

> So far as [Protestant] Christians carrying out religious activities in house-meetings is concerned, in principle they should not be permitted, but they should not be rigidly prohibited. Through work undertaken by the patriotic religious personnel [i.e., the TSPM] to persuade the religious masses, other suitable arrangements should be made.

Because no other unofficial activities of any other religion are singled out, this passage is further indirect confirmation of the growth of the house churches. "Suitable arrangements" is a phrase vague enough to fit all the government control and even closures of house churches over the past three years. In line with its more moderate policies, it is prepared to tolerate worship within the four walls of the designated TSPM churches.

Government control of the church is clearly seen in copies of documents that have been received from two widely separated areas in eastern and western China. The first is a document issued by the RAB and UFWD in a country town in Zhejiang. It refers to a request to set up a church building in the town. It goes on to state that:

> In accordance with the spirit of the constitution, the following persons are named as the working committee for the church in AB village, XY township (names listed). From now on all believers should join this church to conduct normal religious activities. Those meeting points at (3 names listed) and all others in XY township are hereby dissolved. Everyone should go to AB village to meet. It is hoped that the church commit-

tee, under the leadership of the local party members and local government, will arrange religious activities well, without interfering in social order, production, or work schedule.

All believers should strengthen their studies and patriotism and be law-abiding. They should walk the three-self road and obey the four basic principles in order to realize their general responsibilities and contribute to this new phase of socialist modernization.[20]

Although the above document relates to a local situation and does not necessarily describe a nationwide practice, it does indicate the way in which the government's broad principles of prohibiting unregistered house meetings may be implemented. It also shows the influence of the RAB and the UFWD in controlling church activities.

The county from which this particular document was received contains a large number of Christians. The largest group of about 5,000 became the TSPM church. Since January 17, 1984, when this document was issued, two of the other house churches, one with 2,000 and the other with about 500, have continued to hold meetings on Sunday evenings. Some of their members attend the TSPM church on Sunday mornings, hoping to avoid trouble with the authorities. Because the open church is not large enough to contain all the Christians, the authorities up to the present have not objected to the Sunday evening home meetings. Obviously the policy toward independent house churches may vary from place to place, reflecting the attitude of local authorities.

The second example of government control comes from an address by the head of the RAB in Guangxi to TSPM leaders in that province on March 22, 1984. Once again he reiterates the government's intention to use the church as a means to control Christian activity: "We must cause the patriotic church to truly become a religious body with a positive influence to become a bridge for the Party and government to win over, unite and educate religious people . . ." In his subsequent statements he makes very clear that ultimate decision-making power vis-a-vis the church lies not with church leaders, but with the government. This applies even to "spiritual" matters such as baptism.

> Problems can only be solved by the local church *relying on the local government*. For instance, there is the problem of new converts wanting baptism. That is decided by the local church. But what if you are not clear about someone's faith? Or, if there is a need to solve the problem of meeting places? *These questions are decided by the local government* based on concrete conditions. *You* [i.e., the local church leaders] are not able to decide them" (italics ours).[21]

One section of *Document 19* warns Party members that they are not allowed to believe in religion because they are members of a Marxist political party. If, after receiving atheistic education, those who have believed in religion still do not correct their mistakes, they are to be expelled from the Party. Nevertheless there have been many reports in the last few years of CCP officials coming to know the Lord. Truly, God's grace is not limited.

The CCP is concerned with keeping religious activities well within the bounds it has drawn up. Religion as a private matter or as a public cult on certain days is tolerated—but as a vital force affecting the whole of individuals' lives it must be curbed: "We must never allow religion to interfere in the administration of the state, in law, or in schools or social public education." In 1980, one young teacher in Shanghai found himself in trouble for lending his New Testament to his students. He was accused of spreading "anti-socialist ideology" in a government school and was heavily fined.

Teacher or Preacher

Four years ago, a young high school teacher came to know Christ. After two years of Christian life, he was called by a local official from the Education Department, who asked him, "Are you a preacher? Are you a Bible school graduate?"

The teacher answered, "No" to both questions and the official said, "Then why are you preaching? What is your main work?"

The Christian replied, "Teaching mathematics."

The director of the Bureau of Education then said to him, "If you are a teacher you should not be preaching the gospel. How much are you given to preach?"

The teacher said, "No money is given to me, but I give my own money to help the poor."

The Communist official then responded, "I give you three days in which you are to think through this matter and tell me if you are prepared to give up your preaching. Either you must give up your preaching or lose your position as a teacher."

The Christian teacher replied, "I don't need three days. I have a very clear mind. I know and understand the actual situation. I can tell you now that I want to preach. I am also happy to continue my teaching. If I don't teach, it is not that I want to give it up myself. It will be you who force me to give up my teaching. I preach only in my free time."

As a result, this teacher was discharged. Now he is shepherding about 30 groups in the countryside. The leader of the village gave him a piece of land which he has been able to farm very well. He makes good money and continues his preaching.[22]

The CCP, concerned to maintain a complete monopoly of the educational system, does its best to limit religious influences on the young. Evangelization of young people under the age of 18 is forbidden:

> We must never allow the practice of forcing youngsters below the age of eighteen to be converted to some religion or to be sent to temples to be monks or to learn religious scriptures.

To combat the resurgence of interest in religion among young people, the Party wants atheistic propaganda to be intensified. For instance, in December 1983, *China Youth News* called for instruction of youth in atheism, especially elementary school students who needed to be protected "from the harm of superstition and the bad influence of religion."

Children are, however, frequently seen in TSPM church services. One of my friends informed me that he attended a meeting where Christians were told they should not bring their children to church. But in practice the presence of children from Christian homes is tolerated because church leaders realize that if it were forbidden it would alienate the parents whom they are seeking to get to the TSPM church instead of to house meetings.

The Constitution

The new Constitution, which was adopted on December 4, 1982 by the National People's Congress, has an article on freedom of religious belief. Article 36 reads:

> Citizens of the People's Republic of China enjoy freedom of religious belief.
>
> No state organ, public organization or individual may compel citizens to believe in, or not to believe in any religion; nor may they discriminate against citizens who believe in, or do not believe in any religion.
>
> The state protects legitimate religious activities. No one may make use of religion to engage in activities that disrupt public order, impair the health of citizens or interfere with the educational system of the state.
>
> Religious bodies and religious affairs are not subject to any foreign domination.

Previous constitutions contained references to the propagation of atheism and the prohibition of using religion to carry out counterrevolutionary activities. It is encouraging that such stipulations have now been deleted.

Article 36 is much more detailed than the clause in the former Constitution about religious freedom. If put into practice, it should safeguard Chinese Christians from discrimination because of their faith. At the same time, it clearly outlines certain conditions that must be followed in order to enjoy the benefits of religious freedom.

In light of past experience of Communist rule in China, it behooves Christians to pose a few questions concerning the guarantees in the 1982 Constitution, which are open to ambiguity on several counts. For example, will "freedom of religious belief" again be interpreted in such a narrow sense as to prohibit much normal Christian activity? "Normal religious activities" is also a phrase whose interpretation may mean that only those activities undertaken by the TSPM will be viewed with favor. Christians who are otherwise loyal and patriotic may fall outside this category if they continue to meet in their own homes for worship and prayer, and refuse to join the TSPM.

The interpretation and implementation of this crucial phrase was made very clear by TSPM action only one day after the Constitution was passed. On December 5, 1982 the TSPM closed down the largest house church in Guangzhou (200 members) and issued a broadsheet to the church members justifying the action.[23] A pastor who had been leading this flourishing house church for over two years was accused of having:

... privately printed books, and [having] illegally recorded and sold tapes of his sermons. Moreover, he distributed these books and tapes to other places. [He was also accused of allowing] some foreign missionaries to carry out religious activities in his home without the agreement of our China Christian Council, thus harming the sovereignty of our church and disobeying the government's policy.

What is most significant is that Article 36 of the new Constitution is quoted in full to justify the closing of the house church, with the following "explanation" appended:

Therefore stopping X's illegal activities is a powerful measure taken by the government to uphold normal religious activities. We will fully implement this correct expression of the policy of freedom of religious belief.

The broadsheet closes with an exhortation to other house

churches in Guangzhou, described as other "rather abnormal religious activities," to learn from this experience and change their attitude. The message is clear: Only those religious activities approved by the government and the TSPM are "normal." House-church activities in principle do not fall into that category, and pressure was therefore being placed on them either to accept TSPM leadership or to close down. Even though that particular Guangzhou house church has since been reopened, the pattern of events since 1982 shows that, whatever TSPM leadership says publicly to the contrary, both *Document 19* and the Constitution are clearly being interpreted and implemented in a restrictive manner.

The injunction in the Constitution forbidding activities that "impair the health of citizens" may appear to have little connection with religious practices. Yet the government is understandably concerned about the widespread revival of superstitions and witchcraft in the countryside—and Christians may be accused of such practices if they even pray for sick people and lay hands on them.

The ruling that forbids interference with the educational system of the state is relevant to whether young people may be exposed to religious teaching. It is already obvious that the long-range goals of socialist education are regarded as endangered by this.

Christians around the world are thankful for the measure of freedom currently granted by the Chinese government. No longer is Christianity an illegal religion. Therefore, instead of the ruthless persecution that characterized the Cultural Revolution, Christians now face the dangers inherent in the country's growing materialism and legalized religion. As China becomes more prosperous, Christians may be tempted to seek more for material possessions than for the Kingdom of God. As the organized Church gains power and enlarges its influence in the countryside, Christians there may be under pressure to conform and give up their evangelistic zeal.

At the same time, the government will undoubtedly increase its efforts to prevent young people from believing, by emphasizing atheistic teachings in schools. Christians will need to show their support for the government as it seeks to fulfill the Four Modernizations program while at the same time guarding against subtle (or not so subtle) attempts to restrict Church growth.

Clearly, not all of the present governmental policies of restriction and regulation are necessary to the building of a new society. It is evident that Chinese society benefits from the activities of hard-working, honest Christian communities. A government religious policy that seeks to hinder the growth of the Church is not beneficial to the country as a whole. It would be far better for the government to recognize the positive contributions that Christians are making and to acknowledge that Christianity may have a valid part in building up the new China. Although some Chinese officials do see the truth of that statement, there are many whose roots are so deep in Marxism that they regard Christian faith as a serious threat to the basic ideology on which the Chinese government is now built. Others, however, recognize that, in spite of ideological differences, Christians teach respect for authority where Christian conscience is not violated and thus do not constitute a security threat to the state.

HOUSE-CHURCH GROWTH

"I know your works. Behold, I have set before you an open door, which no one is able to shut; I know that you have but little power, and yet you have kept my word and have not denied my name" Revelation 3:8.

The above words were quoted by a small group of Christians who were attending one of the open churches for the first time. One of them came from a place where CIM missionaries first preached the gospel almost 120 years ago. Now, throughout China there has been a tremendous increase in the number of believers— millions of new Christians.

Why so many? The ultimate explanation is the gracious moving of the Spirit of God. A Church purified by suffering has emerged out of intense persecution. Its testimony to the power of God has been made manifest not only in the miraculous transformation of lives, but also in physical and spiritual healing. The collapse of Maoism has created an ideological and spiritual vacuum, as we saw in chapter 4, which in turn has given unprecedented opportunities for the gospel.

In the province of Henan, where Ruth and I worked when we first arrived in China, one county that formerly had 4,000 Christians now has 90,000, with 1,000 meeting places. In that one province alone it is estimated that there may be several million Christians. In Henan, whole villages have become Christian. At Chinese New Year, instead of the traditional sayings on the red strips painted on the door posts, each home has a Christian motto. And Christians have a practical witness as well. In one area, farmers in a non-Christian village complained that the Christian villagers sang hymns and enjoyed themselves on Sundays, working only six days a week. However, the officials to whom they complained replied, "You work seven days, they work six days, but they produce more. In your villages you have problems with theft and other crimes that are not found in the Christian village. So our conclusion is that six is better than seven."

Government officials have recently admitted that in Kaifeng (pop. 600,000), Henan's second-largest city, 10 percent of the people are Christians, compared with only one percent in 1949.[1] In South Gansu, where 40 years ago the progress of the gospel seemed heartbreakingly slow, there are now tens of thousands of Christians.

One small village, where in 1945 were only 10 believers, now has a church of 250 people. In the Northeast, one TSPM pastor reported that there are three times as many Christians in his city as in 1949. In the Northwest, Chinese Christians state, although still small, the Church has multiplied 12-fold during the same period. In the far Southwest, impressive growth has been seen among some of the national minority peoples. But the greatest increase has been in the coastal provinces, especially in that heartland province of Henan, where whole villages have become Christian.

A Spiritual Explosion

We may well ask when this spiritual explosion took place. Before 1978, China was often described as a closed country. It is strange how Christians in the West tend to describe any nation without missionaries as a country closed to the gospel. Actually, in this century, China has never been a closed country. The hearts of Chinese Christians have been open to the work of the Holy Spirit, and the Word of God has gone forth through them.

It is, of course, true that some doors are closed in China; doors are closed to foreign missionaries. The doors of the old church buildings were closed at the time of the Cultural Revolution, which meant the death of the institutional church. But during those 13 years when the visible Church totally disappeared, the seed of the Word of God and the seed of lives laid down for the gospel were bearing much fruit.

The beginning of that spiritual growth was taking place at a time when visitors to China saw only closed doors and were questioning whether the Church would survive. They could not see the little groups meeting in homes, or know that far away in remote country places there were even larger gatherings of Christians. If the Church that survived the Cultural Revolution grew out of those gatherings in homes, we must inquire more carefully into the nature of these "house churches."

Historical Background

House churches are not new in China or in the Church worldwide. Right from apostolic times the gospel has spread not only through preaching in public places, but also through meetings in believers' homes. After Pentecost, the disciples met in homes and broke bread together. After the disciples were beaten and ordered "not to speak in the name of Jesus" they continued teaching and preaching that Jesus was the Christ, both in the Temple and at home. Later, Paul reminded the church in Ephesus how he had been teaching in public as well as from house to house (see Acts 20:20).

As we read church history, we find that house churches have flourished in periods of both revival and persecution. Wesley's class meetings in England and the small groups of persecuted Covenanters in Scotland, who met secretly in homes and mountain caves, are examples of the importance of house meetings.

Before the 1949 Revolution in China, many believers started meeting in homes. I remember in the 1930s taking part in rural evangelistic teams. A co-worker and I lived in a small market town for a month, going out everyday into the thickly-populated countryside to preach in different villages, later returning for an evening meeting in town. Gradually, a small group of Christians was gathered and a meeting started in the home of a believer. After the evangelistic team left, the home meeting continued and a neighboring church sent teachers to help them. Many churches started that way.

House churches in the pre-1949 period were also connected with indigenous movements such as "The Jesus Family," "The True Jesus Church," "The Independent Church" and "The Little Flock." There were hundreds of such Churches throughout the country. They represented many different backgrounds and certainly could not be equated with any one house-church movement in another part of the world. For many years during the Cultural Revolution there was no other Church in China.

Following the 1949 Revolution, the TSPM was responsible for organizing the institutional Church. Indigenous self-propagating churches were suppressed by the TSPM and meetings in homes were declared illegal. In spite of that, many Christians, discouraged by the growing politicization of TSPM churches, risked their liberty by meeting secretly in homes. Then in 1966, all churches were closed, and only small groups that met very unobtrusively survived. For example, a young Christian medical student staying in the home of one of his professors discovered that his instructor too was a Christian. Every week, they would close windows and doors and gather around the Bible to study and pray together. The Bible was one the student had brought from his grandmother's home. Earlier when the Red Guards were searching everywhere for Bibles, his grandmother had diligently wrapped hers in a cloth and hidden it in a flower pot.

In the early 1970s, Christians outside China began to hear of larger meetings in various parts of the country, particularly in the coastal provinces of Fujian and Zhejiang. A friend described how he was meeting for prayer with some other Christians late one night. Through the workings of the Holy Spirit they dedicated themselves to the founding of a church. From that group there gradually grew a house church with as many as 150 people.

A few years ago, this church had 100 new believers applying for baptism. Normally it would have several meetings a week, not only for preaching and worship, but for Bible study, prayer and the training of workers. When they decided to hold baptisms, every meeting of the church except one was used to listen to the new believers' testimonies. Anyone who did not seem clear on his or her faith was later visited by the elders.

Christians in this house church knew they dared not hold a service publicly. A baptistry was built in the courtyard of the house and over it a tent was erected. The day before the baptisms the believers brought water and coals for the fire to heat the water. On the actual day of the baptismal service some people from the TSPM office were looking for the place where the baptisms were being held, but failed to find it—even though baptisms went on from eight o'clock in the morning until late at night. The next day the TSPM representative found the place, and ordered the Christians to turn over a list of those who had been baptized. Such a list once existed, but it had already been destroyed.

This church continued until late 1982, when it was finally forced to disband. Its members, however, are able to keep on meeting in very small secret groups at different times in different homes each week. Occasionally they get together for fellowship in a remote country location. Dividing into smaller groups has meant that they now have more people trained to lead Bible studies.

Reasons for the Growth of House Churches in China

The main factors contributing to the rapid growth of house meetings throughout China are:

1. The breakdown and closure of the institutional Church.

2. The irrepressible desire in the hearts of believers for Christian fellowship.

3. The desire to have their church free from political overtones or government control.

4. The new opportunities for evangelism when Cultural Revolution policies were reversed and Christian meetings were no longer illegal. Through itinerant evangelists, as well as Christians sharing the gospel with relatives and friends, a great harvest of new believers was gathered. One house-church leader in a community of 10,000 saw the church grow from 27 to 550, in just three years. After baptizing 290 in the second year, this

leader was criticized for conducting baptisms when he was not ordained.

(5.) The work of the Holy Spirit bringing revival and manifesting the power of God in healing the sick. In August 1984, a Beijing government newspaper reported that "Christianity fever" was sweeping parts of northern China, commenting that the growing ranks of Chinese Christians who depended on prayer to cure sickness and diseases (in order to avoid paying medical bills!) had become a "serious social problem."[2]

(6.) Christian broadcasting, which has been used to bring many to faith in Christ.

Characteristics of Chinese House Churches

Let us now look at 12 characteristics of house churches in China during recent decades.

(1.) *The house churches are indigenous.*

These house churches are not associated with any organization and certainly have no formal ties with the Church outside China. The vast majority of new believers, since the late '70s, has been the result of indigenous evangelization. Non-Christians realize that many of those who meet in homes are people who passed through times of terrible suffering and maintained their faith with no encouragement from Western Christianity. Thus, they cannot in any sense be associated with Western imperialism.

When the organized churches were destroyed in the Cultural Revolution, traditional forms of Christian ministry were also done away with. The household churches have cast off the trappings of the West and have developed their own forms of ministry, which vary according to their Christian maturity, faithfulness to the Lord, spiritual gifts and soundness of character. The dynamics of house churches, therefore, flow partly from their freedom from institutional and traditional bondage.

Believers from different kinds of ecclesiastical backgrounds have fellowship with each other on a local level. Without any organizational structure, they are not bothered with committee meetings, reports and the power politics so common in large organized churches. They are also free from control by any national organization.

②. *The house churches are rooted in family units.*

House churches have become part of the Chinese social structure. When pressure is placed on the Church, Christians withdraw from large groups and meet in the quietness of homes. During my first return visit to China in 1978, I was told that individuals might believe privately and that the government could not control all that goes on in homes, but any form of open Christian witness was forbidden. In those days many Christians were living very lonely lives, maintaining their faith secretly and taking a risk whenever they gathered with other believers. Even today many Christians, especially among intellectuals, meet only with family members and close friends.

A Christian doctor from China referred to the fact that instead of saying, "Where two or three individuals are gathered together in my name" they say "two or three families." Two more mature Christian families will look for a family that is just approaching Christian faith, or a Christian family that is passing through great testing, and will try to provide support for them. In that way, the believing community is built up with little clusters of Christian families.

A young evangelist who had been encouraging groups of believers in the rural areas of South China recently told me about a training session for house-church leaders. Because he was not authorized to preach by the TSPM, local authorities were keeping an eye out for him. On one occasion he was to lead a training meeting in a house opposite the police station in a small town that was having a Chinese theater performance at the very time they were to meet. Hundreds of theatergoers came on their bicycles and parked them near the theater. Christians joined in the crowd, but slipped away and entered the meeting place by a rear entrance. When the theater let out, the believers again mingled with the crowd, picked up their bicycles, and returned home.

③. *The house churches are stripped of nonessentials.*

Much that we associate with the Church is not found in Chinese house churches today. They have had to exist without buildings, set times of worship or a paid ministry. During the Cultural Revolution and even up to the present, the place of meeting is often changed from one home to another. Even the time is changed to suit the schedules of the Christians as they work at different hours. Thus, the house churches are extremely flexible.

It is difficult for authorities to pinpoint who the leaders are, since the head of whichever home the meeting is held will usually take responsibility for that particular gathering. Christians try to meet in homes with back doors so that people can come and go unnoticed. In addition, the owner has to be a person of good reputation, not under suspicion by the authorities.

Some years ago, when I talked to one young man who had just arrived in Hong Kong, I was surprised to learn that there were no church meetings in his hometown. "How then did you become a Christian?" I asked. He explained that the pastor in his town was under house arrest, but several Christian families lived near him. This young man had come to know Christ through the witness of some of those Christian families; whenever he had questions or was in difficulty he would visit one of their homes. They tithed their money so that whenever someone was in need they would be able to help. Thus, a small group of believers in that town constituted the Church. It had no group worship.

It is Christ who creates the Church, the community in which He lives by His Holy Spirit. Where Christ is in the midst of His disciples, *there* you have the Church. It is *His* presence that gives the Church its authority and power.

4. *The house churches emphasize the lordship of Christ.*

Because Jesus is the head of His body, the Church must place obedience to Him above any other loyalty; it cannot accept control by any outside organization. If that principle is accepted, and the Word of God is obeyed, every attempt to enforce unscriptural practices on the Church will be resisted. The state has the right to demand that Church members should obey laws that are for the good of society, but it must not require Christians to act against their consciences or the principles of the Word of God. The unity of the Church is important, but a united

Church that has lost its purity and its obedience to Christ, will inevitably fail.

The failure of the Church before the Cultural Revolution was due to the fact that it allowed the government to maintain its control. The demand that the Church should take part in political indoctrination, if accepted, was bound to lead to spiritual compromise. The Church put the state above Christ: "Love the country; love the church"—in that order. As long as their faith and conscience are not violated, Christians as individuals should of course fulfill their obligations to the state. But the Church must maintain its independence, its right to be a prophetic voice in society.

(5.) *The house churches have confidence in the sovereignty of God.*

When there was no hope from a human point of view, Christians in China's house churches saw God revealing His power and overruling in the history of their day. God's power was made manifest not when the Church was strong from a worldly point of view, but when the Church was weak, despised and rejected. Christians rejoiced to see God's protection in times of crises.

In one area, at a time when the Church was still facing persecution, almost 5,000 people were baptized. Baptisms took place mainly at night or in some remote place where they could proceed undisturbed. On one occasion when a group of soldiers was sent to interrupt a baptismal service up in the hills, the jeep in which they were traveling broke down on the way. By the time it was repaired, the baptismal service was over and the Christians had scattered to their work in the fields.

On another occasion, a large group of Christians was meeting, very conscious of the Spirit of God. At the end of the meeting five men rose to their feet and announced that they had been sent to make arrests, but they were so moved by what they had seen and heard that they too wanted to believe. The new converts were told to kneel, confess their sins, and receive the gift of salvation in Christ.

There have also been wonderful instances of God's protection in times of danger. A Christian doctor told me that on the night of the Tangshan earthquake, many Christians were among those sleeping in the barracks of a labor camp. One of the guards thought he saw a prisoner escaping over the wall, so he immediately fired off his rifle and alerted the whole camp. The commandant ordered all the inmates to gather outside in an open space in the center of the camp. When the count was taken, it was discovered that one person was missing. Then someone remembered a seriously-ill Christian woman who was not able to walk. She was carried out to the parade ground, and at that moment the earthquake took place, leveling many of the buildings. Because everyone was out in the open, no one was injured or killed.

6. *The house churches love the Word of God.*
House-church Christians appreciate the value of the Scriptures and have sacrificed in order to obtain copies of the Bible. Their knowledge of the Lord has deepened as they have memorized and copied the Word of God. Although Bibles have been printed by the TSPM, the number is inadequate to meet the needs of the large numbers of new believers. In some of the poorer areas, the people lack money to buy Bibles.

A friend of mine went to visit his widowed mother. (His father had been a pastor who died in prison during the Cultural Revolution.) My friend's mother pulled from her dress a scrap of paper with verses of Scripture written on it. "This is my Bible," she said. When she saw the large-character Bible her son had brought for her, she wept for joy.

After he was released from prison in late 1979, Wang Mingdao said that although he had no Bible during those many years, the Bible was in his heart and mind. He told about one prisoner who memorized the entire New Testament.

A Christian woman came from an area where she and her scientist husband were able to have fellowship with only one other Christian family. She described her sadness during the Cultural Revolution when her books, including her Bible, were taken away. Afterward, many of the books were returned, but not the Bible—it was regarded as superstition. Sorrowfully, she realized that she had memorized only the 23rd Psalm. However, in spite of great pressure she had maintained her faith. When she was about to leave China for Hong Kong, she was asked by a cadre whether her thinking had changed.

"If I said yes," she answered, "I would be untrue to myself and untrue to you."

"You are too stubborn," the official responded.

One young man started a "Copy-a-chapter-of-the-Bible-a-day" movement, hiding the manuscripts in the vaults of the government bank where he worked.

A 15-year-old boy wrote to the FEBC saying he had just finished copying the whole New Testament from their 15 minutes of Bible dictation each day.

A young student who registered at a local TSPM church for a Bible had to wait 18 months to receive a copy. Meanwhile, he too took down passages being broadcast over the radio. He also went to the local library where he was able to copy passages from the Word of God, one of its "reference books."

Some Christians wrote out biblical passages, or even the complete New Testament, on stencils and printed them on a local printing press. That was very dangerous, since nothing can be published without government authorization. In 1980 I was told of a man being imprisoned for five years because he had been caught printing a Bible. Even now, believers continue to mimeograph Christian literature because supplies from the TSPM and abroad are so inadequate.

When we were in Henan in 1982, we heard of a young man who came up to a Christian begging for a copy of the Scriptures. The young man knew of 500 new believers without a single Bible. When he was given a Bible he was overjoyed; he knelt on the ground praising God for this precious gift.

Another Christian said when given a few Bibles, "Remember, this is just like bringing a cup of water to put out a forest fire." The need for Bibles was so great.

A final-year medical student who received a Bible, returned two weeks later to the person from whom she got it and asked for another. She explained that she could read hers only four hours a day, since her classmates were reading it the rest of the time.

Study materials and Bible teachers are also greatly needed. In one city during the Cultural Revolution, the Christian young people were organized into areas, with leaders from the different districts coming together for Bible study and training. The person teaching them would never take a Bible to the meeting in case they should be interrupted and thus lose the Bible. Instead, he would copy out the passage to be studied, making extra copies with carbon paper to be shared among the members of the group, who in turn would make other copies. After a few weeks, a whole book of the Bible would have been written and distributed.

The Christian books available, which are very few, and often copied by hand, are in great demand. On a recent journey I gave a book to an old friend whose daughter then spent five hours a night for the next week making copies to share with friends.

Many continue their faith in the Lord Jesus through personal study in their homes. A letter from one young woman contained these words:

> My time for studying is very limited. I hope you will pray for me and ask the Lord to give me intelligence and wisdom, and also to open my heart to understand his Word. It is very precious and we should carefully study it in order to have understanding.

(7.) *The house churches are praying churches.*
During years of weakness and rejection, the Church in China has learned new lessons in the school of prayer. Its existence has depended entirely on God's power. With no human support, and surrounded by those seeking to destroy them, Christians were cast on God, and in simple faith expected God to hear their cry. For the Church in China, prayer was essential to its life. Prayer had to have priority; it was not only communion with God, but was also a way to share in the spiritual conflict. In answer to prayer, the sick were healed, Christians were able to endure suffering and those in danger experienced protection.

Since 1982, the authorities have renewed pressure against the unregistered house churches (see chapter 8). And with that added stress we again hear of Christians entering into a deeper fellowship of prayer. A Christian businessman, reporting on the arrest of several dozen house-church leaders in the city of Xi'an, said, "All we can do is pray and weep for them."[3]

Somewhat earlier, in another location, Christians received notification from the RAB, via the Public Security Bureau, to attend a meeting in the city hall. At that meeting several Catholics and Protestants were standing handcuffed on the platform with their heads bowed. The house-church Christians who had been ordered to attend were accompanied by cadres and police. Members of the TSPM went to the platform and made vehement speeches in support of the arrests.

At the end of the first of what turned out to be a series of meetings, a government cadre announced:

> At present, religious activities are getting out of hand. There are some counterrevolutionary elements in religious "garb" who are carrying out illegal religious activities under cover. Now you must all go home and write out full and frank confessions.

The house-church Christians, expecting to be sent up to the platform to be criticized and possibly arrested, increased their fervent prayer, and covenanted to hold a three-day prayer fast. A few met secretly at night to come before the Lord and pour out their hearts in united prayer.

The following is a translation of one believer's prayer at that time:

> O God, we thank you that you know the difficulties and dangers which your children are encountering. In the midst of these afflictions we confess our sins to you. We ask that you might forgive all the ways great and small in which we have sinned against and resisted you during these past 20 years and have been such poor witnesses to you that your glory has been slighted. Forgive all the brothers and sisters in all the church who have been unfaithful, weak, and defeated before you! We plead that you may forgive all the sins of each one of your servants throughout the Church in China. Forgive also the

offense of the Chinese people as a whole in sinning against you and opposing you.

O God, have these 30 years of suffering which you have used to chasten your children not been enough? We pray that you might put down the rod of chastisement and take away the whip of discipline, for your children are already down before your feet confessing their sins on their knees. We beg that you stretch forth your merciful protective arm to shield your flock!

In the midst of trouble we do accept the discipline you mete out with tears and loud cryings, but O God, if these winds and waves are from you to discipline us, then we will rely upon your bountiful goodness and mercy, asking you that you might abundantly forgive. But if these things come of the enemy's attack, then in your name and in our position as the church standing on your promises, we bind the adversary Satan and destroy all his schemes and threats—we set at liberty your sons and daughters, we set at liberty your church, and in your name we command these winds and waves to be still! Preserve all the members of the Body; let not even one fall or be lost. Let not even one brother or sister be used of Satan!

O Lord, we don't need to go through this kind of persecution again. What the church needs now is the revival that comes in the midst of oppression! We pray that you might protect and strengthen your children and revive your church.[4]

Those who had been accusing the Christians on the first day had spoken forcefully and angrily: "Don't expect to get through this one without confessing and exposing everything. We won't be satisfied with anything less than a complete victory." But after those prayer meetings, the attack stopped. The Christians went home and were never called to another meeting, nor were any confessions or "exposures" required of them. The winds and waves *had* ceased and nothing further happened.

Non-Christians also see the power of prayer in the lives of Christian friends. They have seen firsthand the gospel's power to heal both body and mind. One woman was aware that her Christian neighbors always prayed whenever they faced difficulties. She saw the strength given to them, and the answers to their prayers, and was brought to faith in Christ.

Others have become Christians through healing. In Acts 4:30, *NIV*, we read that the apostles prayed that God would stretch out His hand "to heal and to perform miraculous signs and wonders through the name of your holy servant Jesus." We should not be surprised that God would do the same thing in China.

A group of Christians gathered in one home to pray for a sick member of the family. But soon after, they were interrupted by Communist officials, who asked them what they were doing. The Christians replied and were told that it was illegal to have such a gathering. They were ordered to disperse. One Communist official, however, who in the past had arrested a number of Christians, asked more questions. He was told that in time of trouble or sickness the Christians would pray for one another and seek to help them. He asked if they would be willing to pray for him; he had cancer. The Christians agreed to pray and, as a result, the official was healed, and converted. He was later arrested . . .

Regrettably, it is true that too much emphasis on healing the sick and casting out evil spirits has sometimes resulted in a subjective faith, one that is strong on experience and weak in its understanding of biblical truth. Many know little more than that Jesus has healed their diseases and is able to help them in time of trouble.

(8.) *The house churches are caring and sharing churches.*

A house church is a caring community in which Christians show love for one another and for their fellow countrymen. Such love creates a tremendous force of spontaneous evangelism, even without the usual efforts of organized campaigns.

The Church in China has impressed non-believers with its patience and faithfulness in the midst of suffering. People who have become frustrated and hopeless have seen Christians demonstrating the love of Christ, as they have comforted and upheld those in need.

One way that kind of love has been demonstrated is by taking care of the families of Christians who have been arrested and held for many years. Because food and money are scarce for most of those families, caring for them is an important ministry. To love by sharing one's own means of basic survival takes sacrifice. Because the Chinese live very close in proximity to each other, the neighbors of Christians are aware of what is happening and are often touched by it.

One Christian brother who was imprisoned wrote:

> Since I was separated from the outside world, I could not take care of my family. But the Spirit was at work and moved our brothers and sisters in the Lord to remember us. Some sent me clothes on behalf of my wife in spite of dangers and difficulties. They chose to support me despite insults from others. Others sent money to my wife, fearing that she was in need. What moved me most was that when the political atmosphere all around was extremely tense, and my wife was lying in bed [with spinal tuberculosis] and was unable to feed herself, the Holy Spirit moved an aged sister in the Lord, who herself had great difficulty getting around, to visit her and solve the problem.[5]

In one of the labor camps there was a poor woman who was mentally deranged and in a terrible state. No one had been able to help her. Although she had been sent to doctors, every form of treatment had proved useless. Finally the commandant of the camp asked one of the Christian women to take the ill woman into her room and look after her. The Christian woman lovingly cared and prayed for her new ward, and as a result the patient was completely healed. The knowledge of the love and power of Christ was spread among all the members of that labor camp and now a church has grown up in that area.

While visiting the province of Henan, I was told about a Christian widow who lived with her retarded son in one of the village communes. One day the commune leader happened to come into her home when she was praying. Immediately he told her that since she trusted in God she could expect God to provide for her; the commune would cut off her supplies. The day her food supply was cut off, a woman from another village bought more bread in the market than she needed for her family. On her way home she went to visit the widow, arriving just after she heard the news of her support being cancelled. The visitor was able to share food with the widow, and then returned to her village and spread the news. As a result, Christians in surrounding villages brought food day after day. By the end of the year, the head of the commune was so amazed at the way the woman's needs had been met that he restored her to her rightful place in the commune—and even found a job for her retarded son.

9. *The house churches depend on lay leadership.*

Because so many Chinese pastors were put into prison or work camp, the house churches have had to depend on lay leaders. I asked one who was formerly a house-church leader how leaders are chosen. He replied:

> Every one of the house churches has a little group burdened for the needs of the Church that meets regularly for prayer, and these are really the core of the Church. Out of that little prayer group come forth the leaders. As they pray together, the Lord shows them those who have special gifts and they become the leaders in the Church.

Thus, leadership emerges from the prayer fellowship. Some of those churches spend literally hours in prayer. Country Christians walk for many hours in order to get to the meeting place. After they spend a long time in prayer, they have their service, which is followed by a meal.

In TSPM churches, lay leadership is likely to be much weaker. They have full-time pastors who are supported by government funds (provided by the rent of confiscated church properties).

In the house churches, however, the ministry is made up of people from various walks of life who spend much time going from church to church teaching and building up the faith of others. A Christian doctor, who had been brought up in a Christian orphanage before the Revolution, now in his retirement, travels all over one province contacting those he knew as a child. He reported one county where 6,000 people had come to a faith in Christ. The house churches are not allowed to take up offerings for the support of full-time workers, but the Christians do contribute to those who have been called by God to exercise the ministry of the Word through these faithful visits.

In the past, when pastors and elders have been imprisoned, the work has often been carried on by devoted women. In one place, a young woman was selling her blood to buy paper on which to print Bible study materials. In addition, before her marriage, she made a pact with her fiancé that their wedding gifts of money would be used to buy literature needed for building up the Church. In another case, four women factory workers, poor themselves, gave their extra time to church work. Two used their evenings to make clothing to sell, while the other two wrote Bible study materials and did personal evangelism.

10. *The house churches are in need of biblical teaching.*

House-church leaders in China are very conscious of the failures that have often accompanied the spread of the gospel in rural areas. Wherever rapid church growth occurs, there is likely to be a spiritual counter-attack. Country churches are especially vulnerable and some have erred from their faith because of their lack of Bibles and scriptural teaching.

In one province some believers would accept only the four Gospels, rejecting the rest of the Bible. One man, having read the story of Christ's baptism, insisted that he too must see a dove when he was baptized. Others believed they should pray facing Jerusalem. When teaching is incomplete, heresies can enter. Reports have been received of syncretism in some places, where Buddhist beliefs and Chinese folklore have been combined with Christian teaching.

Some Christians have been led astray by extreme teaching of one kind or another. A teacher who claims to have a special brand of truth that makes his people "superior" to others can have many followers.

In some areas, Christians have been divided by teaching given by groups claiming that they alone represent the true Church. One such group was receiving Bibles from the outside that were intended for general distribution. Nonetheless, they refused to give out those Bibles to Christians, unless they joined *their* group. They were very strong in their attacks on other Christian brothers and sisters. Later, when some of their leaders were arrested by the government, other Christians went to minister to those among them who were left with no pastoral care.

Since 1983, the government, in cooperation with the TSPM, has waged a widespread campaign against Christians who belong to a group known as The Shouters. Their name comes from their practice of shouting in unison "Jesus is Lord." They also shout passages of Scripture. The government claims that they are followers of Witness Li, who for the past few years has been in America as the leader of a group known as The Local Church. Li's group has churches in many parts of the world, with the largest numbers found in Taiwan. A Chinese government document with the title, "Actively strike down the leading elements of the counterrevolutionary organization 'The Shouters,'" describes the charges against seven men who had been arrested. In addition to being charged with political crimes, it was stated that they "have sent information abroad, received foreign aid, and printed, distributed and broadcast foreign reactionary books and tapes."

Not all of the seven arrested were linked with the followers of Witness Li. It seems that The Shouters has now become almost a generic term that includes many different types of house-church people. Those arrested may come from The Local Church, pentecostal groups, or are house-church members who have stated their opposition to joining the TSPM. One Christian woman who was caught entertaining members of The Shouters in her home had to write a letter of repentance and arrange for 1,000 copies to be printed and posted throughout the county, at her own expense (see Appendix 5). Across the country, the

TSPM has conducted seminars to denounce The Shouters and has published a book by Tang Shoulin describing what they consider to be doctrinal errors.[6]

In view of the danger of false teaching, one of the great needs is to find people who are able to give true scriptural teaching. The work of the Holy Spirit in preparing lay leadership is seen in the experience of a young man who discovered a Bible in the home of an old woman and started reading it. Soon gripped by the Word of God, he returned again and again to read this precious book. The old woman, becoming nervous about his visits, finally allowed him to take the Bible. Through his reading he came to know Christ. Then he found a little house meeting nearby, and through fellowship with other believers he grew in the knowledge of Christ.

When persecution in that area subsided, he discovered many new believers, but no teachers. The pastor had been imprisoned. Bibles were scarce. He decided that there ought to be some kind of simple teaching aid for new believers, and began writing a little book on the main doctrines of the faith. His non-Christian wife discovered his manuscript, however, and, afraid that it would get them into trouble, she threw it into the fire. After several more attempts over a period of years to write such a book, he succeeded. His manuscript was duplicated on stencils and distributed to thousands of new Christians in the area. By then his wife had been converted as a result of listening to Christian broadcasts on the radio.

Later when the pastor was released from prison, this man showed him and other church leaders his little book. They were tremendously impressed by what he had written, and felt there was clear evidence that God had been leading him. They laid their hands on him, prayed for him and then sent him back to continue his ministry.

11. *The house churches have been purified by suffering.*

The Church in China has learned firsthand that suffering is part of God's purpose in building His Church. Writing about the difficult days of the Cultural Revolution, one Christian brother said, "Christians dared not speak to each other. They went about with a heavy burden on their backs so to speak." They were rejected and despised, and some of them broke down under the pressure. Some denied their Lord and betrayed fellow Christians. Yet from those days of awful anguish, God brought forth a renewed Church. In Acts 14:22, Paul exhorted the disciples to continue in the faith; it is through many tribulations, he said, that we enter the Kingdom of God.

Suffering in the Church in China has worked to purify it. Nominal Christianity could not have survived the tests of the Cultural Revolution. Because those who joined the Church were aware that it was likely to mean suffering, their motivation had to be a *genuine* desire to know Jesus Christ. Several people have stated that there are no longer nominal believers who join the Church for material benefit ("rice Christians"). We used to speak of those who were *you ming wu shi*, meaning "having a name but no reality." Only those who have real faith and are prepared to take the consequences now identify themselves as Christians.

Suffering provides evidence of the reality of faith. One woman who had been through a great deal of difficulty because of her faith was heard to have remarked, "In China if a person joins us we have a real Christian, but in Hong Kong we are not so sure."

A Chinese doctor wrote, "I do not speak about the suffering of the Church but of the purifying of the Church." Most of the leaders who are trusted today have spent long years in prison or labor camps. They have been through intense indoctrination; some have been beaten. All experienced total rejection and humiliation during the Cultural Revolution. Yet they do not express antagonism, resentment or bitterness. They love their country and are doing their best to serve others.

The suffering endured by Christians in China has enabled them to draw closer to non-Christians, especially to intellectuals, who were also going through suffering. Often that gave them opportunity to witness to God's grace in the midst of their shared trouble. Certainly the suffering experienced during the Cultural Revolution prepared the hearts of many to seek true meaning to life.

Believers are still suffering in China. One letter written from Henan province in January 1984 reads:

Brother *X* was injured when he was beaten with a pistol by the head of the RAB while he was being interrogated . . . . There are also two sisters who are now in prison.

Another from the same area reports:

I have been released on bail and returned home. Twenty-nine others have all been released on bail and returned home. But another brother was interrogated at night and tortured severely. He was sent back to his dormitory but then he disappeared. I've been making inquiries but don't know what has happened to him.

(12.) *The house churches are zealous in evangelism.*

During the last decades, the Church in China has learned new lessons in evangelism. There was a tendency in the past to depend on mass evangelistic meetings and on trained workers with elaborate equipment to proclaim the gospel from the pulpit. Then for over 10 years, no public preaching was allowed. People came to know Christ through the humble service of believers and through intimate contact between friends or family members. They learned that the Church could grow through personal friendship and by the sincere one-to-one sharing of faith.

The main method of witness in China today is through the personal life-style and behavior of Christians, accompanied by their proclamation of the gospel, often at great personal risk.

Some years ago, one of my Chinese friends staying in a city hotel was much impressed by the attitude of a woman who was sweeping the floors. One day, finding her alone, he asked if she was a Christian. She replied that she was, and added, "I cannot say much about my faith, but I seek to show my love to others. And sometimes when people ask me, I can talk about the Lord Jesus."

One high school student had picked up many bad habits through association with an urban gang. His parents, who were government officials, were very concerned about him. One day, needing to see his teacher about some schoolwork, the student arrived at the teacher's house while a Christian meeting was taking place. At first the teacher was reluctant to let him in, but after consulting with the other Christians decided to invite the student to join them. That day, he heard the gospel and was converted. His parents noticed the change in his life, and one day his father entered his room and found him reading the Bible.

"Oh," he said, "is this the reason for the difference in your behavior? How did you come to get this Bible?"

"My teacher gave it to me," the young man replied and told how he had become a Christian. To his surprise, his father said, "You must invite your teacher to visit our home." As a result, the Christian teacher was able to share the message of Christ with the whole family, and at least one other family member became a Christian.

People noticed the kindness a Christian doctor showed to those who belonged to the class known as "nondesirables." During the Cultural Revolution at least five percent of the population was classified as belonging to the "seven bad elements": landlords, capitalists, rich peasants, rightists, counterrevolutionary elements, bourgeoisie and gangsters. All those groups were discriminated against in many different ways, so the Christian doctor's kindness to "nondesirables" was especially noteworthy.

Suffering was also a means of witness to non-Christians. A young girl working in a factory during the Cultural Revolution was very much impressed by the way in which the chief engineeer, who was a Christian, suffered for his faith. When the Red Guards saw him giving thanks for his food, he was badly beaten and deprived of food for three days. At the end of that period, he was offered dirty food picked up off the floor. Again he gave thanks. They asked him why he thanked God for such food, and he replied that he thanked God that he was still able to eat. It was not the right answer; again he was beaten. The young girl went home and told her brother the story.

Sometime later, the brother found himself sharing a room with a Christian doctor. Once, when the young man had taken ill, the doctor lovingly cared for him. One day he asked the doctor, "Do you really believe in God?" The doctor explained why he believed in God and then the youth told him the story he had heard from his sister. "All my family are CCP members," he said, "but the witness of that engineer made a big impression on me, and now I have met you and you have told me of your faith in God." As a result that young man came to know Jesus Christ.

One Christian told about her brother-in-law who was in a labor camp for many years. Originally his sentence had been 10 years, but at the end of that time it was said that his thinking had not changed and he was given another 10 years. (After 1978 he was released.) Someone who sympathized with her because of her brother-in-law's long imprisonment was told, "Don't be sorry. How else could the people in that labor camp hear about the Lord Jesus?"

In one country church the leader was a man who had once been a Party secretary, captain in the local militia and leader of a farm production battalion. After he became a Christian, he was imprisoned for several years. At the close of one meeting he knelt on the ground and begged the other Christians to have one heart in serving the Lord. He said,

> We have traveled nine out of ten miles. There is yet one mile ahead of us. Let us proclaim the gospel and satisfy the heart of our Lord. Let us not forget the great commission that the Lord gave to His disciples after He rose from the dead. He has also commissioned us who live in the last days to be faithful servants of Christ.[7]

As a result of that meeting the church sent out 13 teams to preach the gospel. One group consisted of 14 persons, the youngest, a girl only 16 years old. Sometimes this group preached on the streets and in one month an estimated 5,000 people heard their message. Because of their enthusiasm and love for the Lord, these 14 young preachers were arrested. They were forced to kneel on the ground for three days and three nights with their arms and legs tightly bound.

Many other house churches have missionary vision, displaying courageous evangelistic zeal as they try to make the message known in areas where the gospel has not yet been preached.

Jesus Christ promised in Matthew 16:18, "I will build my

church, and the powers of death shall not prevail against it."
Through the work of the Holy Spirit He is giving spiritual gifts—
the calling and ability to be prophets, evangelists, pastors and
teachers—to equip His followers to build up His Church. We can
be confident that in spite of all the dangers that may lie ahead,
the witness to our living Lord will continue.

THE THREE-SELF PATRIOTIC MOVEMENT

In the early days of the Cultural Revolution, when the last church in Shanghai was closed, the *South China Morning Post* in Hong Kong carried a headline announcing "The Last Chapter in the Church in China." For 13 years there was no public worship in Shanghai. But in September 1979, the large church formerly known as Moore Memorial Church opened its doors with the new name *Mu-en Tang* (Bathed in Grace Church). In the very early hours of that first Sunday when it had been announced that services would be held, groups of Christians could be seen wending their way to the large church building, that was still used as a school during the week.

Arrangements for the opening of the church were made by the Three-Self Patriotic Movement, which is responsible to the Religious Affairs Bureau and serves as a liaison between the government and the churches. It is not a church in itself, but all relationships between churches and state must be channeled through it. Its constitution makes explicit the mingling of political and religious aims in the movement.[1] Its main duties are to insure that the government's policy on religion is understood and obeyed by TSPM workers and ordinary believers, to unite all Christians under its leadership and to arrange for both Christian and political education of church workers and members. Up to the present, in order to implement those policies, the TSPM has not gone to the extremes seen in the 1950s.

In 1979 the TSPM had practically no influence among the

thousands of house churches, and the great numbers of new believers had never even heard of it. TSPM leaders recognized that their organization was able to affect only the small numbers of newly-opened churches in the buildings restored by the government. Their first goal, therefore, was to extend their influence and to gain acceptance among the independent house churches; only then could they begin to organize those churches according to government policy.

TSPM Claims and Problems

In order to establish their credibility, the TSPM leaders made three claims:

1. They insisted that they represented the truly patriotic Christians.

> Today, no matter where we Chinese Christians meet, the overwhelming majority supports the People's liberation movement heartily. We give thanks to God in our prayers for the achievements of socialist new China. We are all willing to make our contributions to the Four Modernizations of our country.[2]

2. The TSPM took credit for removing from the Church the stigma of being a foreign religion. Bishop Ding stated:

> Today Christianity in China has by and large rid itself of the control and exploitation of imperialism, bureaucratic capitalism, and feudalism . . . . It is no longer dependent on foreign missionary societies but is organized by a part of the Chinese citizenry out of our faith and love of Christ.
>
> In the eyes of an increasing number of our compatriots, Christianity is no longer a foreign religion and Christians are no longer looked upon as "foreign worshiping" or mere "rice Christians."[3]

We can readily understand the emphasis on the independence of the Church in China and are thankful that Christianity is no longer regarded as a foreign religion. But the indigenous nature of the Chinese Church and its survival are surely due not to the pronouncements of TSPM leaders, but to the truly "three-self" principles manifest in the independent house churches. They have supported their own workers, managed their own affairs, and actively spread the gospel in unevangelized areas. Their leaders have not asked for the return of Western missionaries, although they have welcomed fellowship with the Church overseas: their prayer support, provision of literature and Christian radio programs.

It is good then that responsibility for the evangelization of China should be in the hands of the Chinese Church. Who would want to see an invasion of Western religious organizations competing in China for areas of influence? Chinese Christians are concerned about the needs of their society, and house-church members have indeed demonstrated their love and concern for their country.

3. The TSPM pointed to the fact that reopening of old church buildings, provision of paper for Bibles and permission to print Christian literature could be gained only through their organization.

However, TSPM leaders faced four problems:

1. *Restoration of church buildings.* Church buildings now occupied by government agencies needed to be reclaimed and restored for worship services. Because of the shortage of buildings it was not easy to find other accommodations for the present occupants. During the first year, only a few churches in the major cities were opened. Later, the number being opened each month increased rapidly.

2. *Provision of pastors.* Most of the pastors available were men between 60 and 80 years of age, almost all former TSPM pastors from the 1950s. Because there are no longer denominations in China, most of the reopened churches had a team of pastoral workers that reflected different denominational backgrounds.

3. *Gaining the confidence of Christians.* Because of the extreme politicization of the Church and the persecution in the

earlier years of Christians who would not join the TSPM, those who had been worshiping in house churches were now reluctant to join. Arne Sovik of the Lutheran World Federation wrote in 1979:

> The Three-Self Movement is likely to have some difficulty in unifying the Protestant community . . . [it] tends to be seen by many groups as a political rather than a religious instrument. The tension that is the heritage of the accusation meetings and of the differences between the "faithful" and the Christians who compromised or left the faith during the Cultural Revolution period has already created a problem reminiscent of the Donatist controversy of the fourth century church. As long as these memories last, there is likely to be either great reluctance to develop a unified Protestantism or a tendency toward something analogous to the Baptist churches of the Soviet Union, where unrecognized groups live in insecurity and there is some suspicion of the recognized church which has accepted government registration. If in the last generation the western denominational differences have broken down, there seems to be evidence of a threat of other divisions, the result of theological differences to be sure, but also of different responses to the problem of life in socialist China.[4]

Before the Cultural Revolution, the leaders of the TSPM had been very liberal in their theology. That was one reason they were so strongly opposed by many evangelical pastors. Now, however, those leaders have recognized that both the Christians who survived the Cultural Revolution and the new believers are nearly all evangelical in faith; they could not expect such people to come to TSPM churches to hear liberal and political sermons. So, to broaden their appeal among the Christian masses, the TSPM has instructed pastors to preach from the Bible. Theologically-liberal and politically-oriented sermons are no longer the norm. Efforts have been made to include known evangelicals in the pastoral team of the churches.

The Forming of the China Christian Council

Further, because the leadership was aware of the suspicion attached to TSPM in the eyes of Chinese evangelical believers, another "gear" was added to smooth the workings between the Communist state and the Christian Church. This new organization is the China Christian Council (CCC), formally brought into existence in October 1980. Its constitution has a more spiritual note than that of its parent body.[5] The relationship of the CCC to the TSPM is one of "division of labor." In administration and leadership, however, it remains intimately associated with the TSPM, and Bishop Ding chairs both organizations.[6]

The tasks of the CCC are more directly religious and pastoral than those of the TSPM, being specifically the:

> Supervision of the work of churches and priests, training of candidates for the Christian ministry, publishing the Bible and other devotional materials, and strengthening contacts among all churches and believers in China.[7]

4. *Need for biblical teaching.* A new generation of pastors and teachers was desperately needed. So, in March 1981, the TSPM reopened the Nanjing Theological Seminary. It started classes with 47 students drawn from about 1,000 who had applied and taken examinations in various areas of China. For the second term the number of students increased to 51 between the ages of 17 and 35. By 1984, the enrollment was up to 185, one-third of which were women.

Correspondence courses and short-term Bible schools have also been used to give the teaching that is so urgently needed. Reports of training classes being held, as well as evening courses for working people, have come from many parts of the country. Materials used in these training classes, including a well-written catechism published by the CCC and a book of excellent sermons, are orthodox in theology. Four other seminaries have been opened and two new schools, one for minority nationalities in Yunnan or Sichuan and one for the southcentral region in Wuhan, were being planned for 1985.

International Relations

The leaders of the TSPM were also concerned about reestablishing contacts with the Church outside China. In September 1979, some TSPM delegates participated in a world conference of religion and peace in Princeton, New Jersey. That was the first of a series of overseas delegations seeking to restore relations with the worldwide Church. The first visits were all related to the liberal wing of the Church, but more recently efforts have been made to establish contact with evangelicals, even to the extent of cooperating in a Bible conference for Christians from America in Tianjin in July 1984.

National Conference 1980

After a lapse of more than 10 years, the standing committee of the TSPM met in Shanghai in March 1980. An open letter sent to all parts of the country was addressed to "Brothers and Sisters in Christ" and expressed gratitude for the fact that:

> Our witness to Christ has not been dimmed but has achieved a great deal in the course of the past 30 years. As a result of this movement, more and more Chinese Christians have come to cherish our homeland . . . Chinese Christianity is no longer a tool exploited by imperialism or by other reactionary forces . . . it is no longer a foreign religion . . . but is a religion governed, supported, and nurtured by Chinese Christians.

In the 1950s, both Bishop Ding and other TSPM leaders were extremely opposed to evangelicals. Of the members of the 1980 standing committees of the TSPM and CCC, however, three were described as "evangelical Protestants." In addition to them, Tang Shoulin is described as "a leader of the former Little Flock," and he has been used by the TSPM to appeal to former

"Little Flock" members, the followers of Watchman Nee.[8] Later, he cooperated with another TSPM leader to write a book exposing the errors of "the Shouters." It seems that those evangelical leaders who join the TSPM are expected publicly to announce their acceptance of TSPM attitudes and policies.

During the 1980 national conference, Bishop Ding made it plain that the TSPM was not content to relate only to the small minority of Christians who attended TSPM churches. He insisted that those who worshiped in homes were just as much a part of the Church. At that time, many Christians were encouraged by the apparent legal status given to house-church Christians, and for almost two years the house churches took full advantage of the recognition granted them.

It soon became clear, however, that the real purpose was to draw all Christians into the CCC and TSPM. Since March 1982, when the CCP definitely stated in its internal party document on religion that the house churches should, in principle, be prohibited, the attitude of the government and of the TSPM appears to have hardened. Many house-church leaders were arrested in late 1983, and although by mid-1984 some had been released, it is evident that neither the Party nor the TSPM is willing to tolerate the existence of a flourishing, independent house-church movement.

At the same time, great efforts have been made to strengthen the TSPM organization throughout the country. National, provincial, county and city committees were set up. Everywhere the independent house churches have been urged to join the TSPM.

As we saw in chapter 5, there is no basic difference between the religious policies of the Communist Party at the top level and those of the TSPM at the lower levels. Their common purpose is further confirmed by various internal TSPM documents. For example, a document entitled "Decisions Regarding the Safeguarding of Normal Religious Activity" was promulgated in Yunnan in March 1982 (see Appendix 4). This document pertains to the "Three Designates" for the control of the Church, which were later approved by Jiao Liansheng, head of the RAB, in a speech in Beijing in September 1982. The Three Designates are: designated places of worship, designated pastoral personnel and a designated sphere for pastoral activities.

The first of those requirements is expressed in the Yunnan document as: "The ministerial activities and religious activities of each church should all be conducted inside the church buildings." The aim is to persuade Christians to worship only in places that are registered with the TSPM, which could include recognized house-church meetings.

Second, all religious workers must be registered by the TSPM, including those who have been ministering in house churches. The government is strongly opposed to unauthorized evangelists or teams of volunteer workers going from place to place preaching the gospel.

The third designate concerns the sphere of activities of recognized ministers. Evangelists or pastors are not to go to unevangelized areas but are to remain in the place of their appointment. In one city several years ago, an evangelical pastor. wished to take the gospel message to unreached peoples. Not being able to do so himself, he encouraged young people in the church to go.

At the present time, however, only Christian workers specifically authorized by the TSPM can be sent to places outside their own district. The head of the RAB in Guangxi, speaking to TSPM leaders on March 22, 1984, made this quite clear. He referred to some TSPM pastors in Liuzhou City who "went to neighboring counties to make some converts" and said, "This is actually illegal." He went on to say that if believers in a neighboring area requested help in holding religious services, the Church could make a proposal and then:

> The relevant religious departments of the municipal and county people's government can discuss this; cities and towns with religious personnel can designate certain pastors to go to local churches for a fixed period to hold religious services and preach. *Other people cannot cross boundaries and undertake evangelism as they please* (italics ours).

Reports have been received about the way in which the TSPM cooperates with the Public Security Bureau to arrest independent preachers. This practice is confirmed by the final section of the Yunnan document, which reads:

> All who transgress the above decisions should undergo re-education, and if they have not changed after re-education, the relevant department of the government can be requested to deal with them.

In contrast to the autonomy and lack of organization in the house churches, the TSPM has achieved considerable success in building up an institutionalized Church. At the end of 1980 TSPM had opened only about 30 churches. By June 1984 that number increased to 1,800, a figure that undoubtedly includes many churches that formerly were independent. Of those 1,800 churches, 920 are in Fujian and Zhejiang. Shanghai has 18 churches, in contrast to 200 in 1949. Ordination services have been held in many centers, with women as well as men being ordained.

The Four Types of Churches in China

A house-church leader listed the churches in China as belonging to four types.[9] First there are the worship halls *(libai tang)* often called the "open churches," which have been opened under the aegis (sponsorship) of the TSPM.

Closely associated with them are thousands of meeting points *(juhui dian)*. These are meetings in homes, usually pre-dating the worship halls, which have now registered with the TSPM. A TSPM pastor may go to speak at such meetings on a monthly basis, and their leaders will be called to attend TSPM training courses.

A third type is the house meeting *(jiating juhui)*, in places where formerly there was no TSPM church. They have now registered with the nearest TSPM local committee, but appoint their own pastors and generally have little contact with TSPM, except for the times when their leaders must attend TSPM meetings.

Last are the free (or independent) house meetings *(ziyou jiating juhui)*, which are not registered with the TSPM. In more remote country regions these meetings may be quite large, but in both town and country areas within easy reach of TSPM committees, they are likely to be small, and secret.

The house-church leader who gave this report belonged to the third type of meeting. He had traveled widely in 13 provinces.

Before 1982 very few of the house churches were registered with TSPM. At the present time it is hard to know how many have joined. Some groups declare that they are "Three-Self" because they agree with the basic Three-Self principles, but as far as possible they avoid contact with the organization.

Recent letters from groups of Christians in two large cities still voiced very strong opposition to association with TSPM. A Chinese pastor who had just returned from a visit to China where he met a number of independent church leaders, told me that in one city with many Christians and many churches that are claimed by TSPM, the work of TSPM is confined to an office. The Christians have as little contact as possible with this office, and are greatly disturbed by the fact that a TSPM pastor works with the police in searching out church leaders who will not cooperate.

But there are also Christians who feel that they can have a ministry among the large numbers who attend churches associated with TSPM. Among the crowds thronging these churches are a number of different types of people.

First are older people who are full of rejoicing that once again they can go to church. An elderly lady told my wife, "I am 86, and now I can go to church again." After years of being deprived of any opportunity for corporate worship, they are glad to be able to sing familiar hymns and take part in Sunday services. Many of them have suffered in the past.

Second are those who have become Christians during or shortly after the Cultural Revolution. They have been invited by friends to join in services at the TSPM church.

Third are the very new Christians who are just beginning to understand the meaning of the Christian faith. They know little first-hand of the trauma of the Cultural Revolution and have even less understanding of the past suffering of believers in China.

Fourth are many who are curious and only go to church to see what is going on. Some are dissatisfied with Marxist ideology and think that perhaps in the church they will find something to fill the spiritual void in their lives.

Fifth are informers in the churches. These informers are not concerned about older people, but are looking for students and young people who attend and then often report them to their school or work unit. Young people may have a difficult time when confronted with the fact that they have been to church. One young man who attended a church in a rural area was sent to the city by his unit to buy supplies. Because he was there on a Sunday he went to the church and had a short talk with the pastor. Once he got back he was amazed to find two local plain-clothes people from the PSB waiting to question him. He was also called out by the head of his unit and strongly reprimanded for going to the church.

In another instance, a young woman had obtained permission to visit relatives in America. Knowing they were Christians, she decided that it would be a good thing for her to visit one of the TSPM churches before she went to see her family. Two days later at the weekly meeting of her unit, to her amazement and fright, she was confronted with the fact that she had been to church, and was told by her leader that many "bad elements" were still in the church and it was very wrong for her to go.

Again, the cooperation between the church and the PSB is evidenced in the experience of another young Christian woman. She had met a Western student at the church, and later, she and a friend were seen talking with him in a park. When the young man left, a policeman came and questioned the two girls. The young Christian woman said she was a member of the church and it was perfectly natural for her to speak to a fellow Christian. The police officer, however, reported her to the church, and sent a report naming her Western friend to his unit. Later, the young woman was reprimanded by the pastor. She insisted that there was nothing wrong in talking with a fellow believer who came from another country, but pressure was put on her everytime she went to the church. Eventually, she had to cut off all contact with this new Christian friend. In other places, along this same line, worshipers in certain churches have been discouraged from having anything more than superficial conversations with foreign visitors who attend.

Among the pastors serving in these churches, are some strong evangelicals; others are primarily political. Frequently they have had a liberal theological background. They would echo the words of a member of a TSPM delegation visiting England who, when asked if he emphasized the political or the spiritual, replied, "We're 100 percent spiritual and 100 percent political."

In one church I attended, I noticed a difference in the congregation's response to different pastors. When one pastor who was known and loved was leading in prayer, there was a chorus of "Amens" from all across the congregation. A friend told me about a service in another place in which the pastor gave a short biblical introduction and then started on a political message. Someone was heard to have whispered, "Now we have the politics." In some cities where there is more than one TSPM church, some young believers try to discover who is speaking on a particular Sunday in each church and then go where they can get the most spiritual food.

An evangelical pastor talked about the tension that developed because of the political activities of one member of the pastoral team. During one service, a church member became so disgusted because of the political message being given that he walked out, went upstairs and prayed until the sermon finished. After the service he joined in a fellowship meeting and announced, "If the pastor knows the Bible and does not preach the Bible, he commits sin."

Some pastors who served the TSPM in the 1950s went through great suffering at the time of the Cultural Revolution. In some cases they were revived in faith and purified by that experience.

As has been said, there are also pastors well known for their evangelical faith. Sometimes they have been active in the independent house churches but have now been persuaded to join the TSPM, feeling they have a responsibility to maintain an evangelical witness in those circles.

One believer wrote to tell me of his joy when he was invited to join the staff of a newly-opened church. He had suffered greatly during the Cultural Revolution and had, in fact, been very strongly criticized by TSPM leaders. After being rehabilitated, he worked in a factory and had almost given up hope of ever being able to preach again. A committed Christian can understand the joy he experienced when, after reaching retirement age, he was allowed to stand once again in the pulpit and teach from the Scriptures. In a recent letter this pastor wrote about a midweek Bible study in that church in which nearly 100 people attend.

Agonizing Decisions

We cannot enter into the spiritual conflict in China today, unless we can understand the agonizing decisions that Chinese Christians have to make. We must show prayerful concern for those who believe that God has called them to work in the TSPM churches, understanding their thankfulness that the government allows a measure of freedom and also their desire to have a public witness.

But we must likewise appreciate the thinking of those who urge us to look beyond the great crowds in the TSPM churches and think of the dangers facing a church that conforms completely to government demands. Most Chinese do not accept all the statements made by the government, and it would be foolish to take at face value all the reports given by TSPM spokesmen.

What will be the long-term effect of the growing control of the Church by the TSPM? Does it result in a dilution of its message and a shackling of those who are zealous to proclaim the gospel in unreached areas? If we are to empathize with fellow members of the Body of Christ, we must listen both to those who work within the official Church and to those who object so strongly to what they regard as the compromise of basic principles.

In Favor of Joining TSPM

As already noted, the numbers of those who have joined TSPM-related churches have increased in recent years. There are several reasons for such a development.

1. *To gain legality.* Some house groups have joined in order to gain legality for their gatherings. They would say that in a Communist state they cannot expect any organization to be free from government supervision. Because unauthorized meetings, whether inside or outside the church, are always considered subversive, many Christians fear that if they remain outside the TSPM they will be regarded as counterrevolutionary and will ultimately face persecution. They believe they should take advantage of the freedoms given to those who follow the TSPM's lead.

2. *To witness publicly.* Some Chinese Christians see a church recognized by the government as an opportunity for public witness. They can demonstrate the fact that Christian faith is neither an illegal nor a foreign religion.

3. *To encourage inquirers.* TSPM churches provide a meeting place where curious young people can go to find out about the Christian faith. Although often frustrated by the restrictions placed on the church, some who join the TSPM believe nonetheless that TSPM-registered churches provide an important opportunity for evangelism. It is not easy to invite non-Christians to secret house-meetings, whereas the invitation to attend large churches where there are great crowds of people is not nearly so threatening.

4. *To minister to new believers.* Some Christians see the TSPM churches as places where they can minister to new believers. They realize that many who go to those churches have little understanding of the Christian faith and need people who can explain the gospel to them. They may find opportunities to lead Bible study groups or assist in the production of a limited amount of Christian literature.

5. *To connect with the "life of the vine."* Some who are very unhappy about the TSPM's top leadership still feel that the

TSPM is like a trellis on which the true vine may grow. One said to me, "The trellis may be dead, but the vine has life."

Further, only through membership in that organization can they get back the old church buildings and obtain government permission to print the Bible. In addition to 1 million Chinese Bibles, the TSPM has also printed Korean, Lisu and Miao versions of the Scriptures. A hymnbook with 400 hymns, a catechism, a Christian magazine and some teaching materials, although limited, have also been published through the TSPM.

The TSPM is also able to provide a channel for the disbursement of government funds obtained through the rental of church property. In addition, its liaison with the government enables it to protest if local officials persecute Christians in their area. Even though evangelicals may be pessimistic about the future of the TSPM because of its present leadership, some of them still think it is important to maintain a witness within the church and to seek to overcome the various forms of false teaching that threaten the purity of Christian witness in China.

Opposition to Joining TSPM

Those who refuse to join the TSPM, on the other hand, believe they have very strong justification for taking that position.

1. *Undermining of loyalty to Christ.* Many Christians are convinced that the government exercises ultimate authority within the TSPM churches; Christ is no longer head of the Church and therefore it is not the true Church. They claim that politically-minded people control the appointment of pastors, and that spiritual qualifications and the guidance of the Holy Spirit are not given their true place in the choosing of leaders.

2. *Government control of teaching.* Many believe that the TSPM accepts suggestions made by the government that are contrary to Scripture. The TSPM insists that the teaching given in the church is not in any way controlled by the government. However, it is a fact that the government's objection to any teaching against believers marrying unbelievers has resulted in the church's refraining from giving such instruction.

Further, although pastors are not explicitly forbidden to preach about the Second Coming, it is well known that the government does not favor such teaching. Pastors may also get into trouble if they discuss the apocalyptic teaching of Daniel and Revelation, although some continue to preach from these books. The government also frowns on what is described as "pushing the gospel," which means openly seeking to introduce it to non-Christians outside regular church activities within registered buildings, or to preach and distribute tracts in public places. This does not, of course, prohibit the private sharing of the gospel within the home.

3. *TSPM's past history.* Older Christians point to the fact that in the 1950s some evangelical pastors spent years in prison because they refused to join the TSPM. (Many of the leaders who persecuted Christians during that period are still in the top echelons.) The spiritual life of the Church was dying, evangelical ministry was being destroyed and both the numbers attending the churches and the numbers of churches being opened were decreasing rapidly. It seemed that by using the TSPM to control the Church, the government was effectively preventing the spread of Christian faith. Could that happen again?

4. *Limited opportunities for evangelism.* Restrictions continue to limit opportunities for evangelism. Bishop Ding has stated:

> Our evangelism does not have as its only or main target the number of converts . . . . Today, as far as numbers are concerned, a conservative estimate of baptized non-Roman Christians in China would be around two million, i.e., three times that of 1949. We do not think this big numerical growth should or can continue, because it is already larger than our work of Christian nurture can cope with.[10]

Since then Bishop Ding has raised his estimate to 3 million. Those opposed to joining TSPM point to the effect on evangelism of some of the regulations already published by local TSPM organizations, as in Yunnan (Appendix 4).

5. *Use of the church for political indoctrination.* Many house-

church Christians, while recognizing their responsibility to obey the rules of the country and to contribute to the building up of the new China, are totally opposed to the use of the Church for political indoctrination. They are firmly convinced that some of the TSPM top leaders are serving the government rather than Christ. They strongly object to phrases in the Yunnan Document such as "Christians must uphold the Four Basic Principles." Those principles are: "the socialist road; the people's democratic dictatorship; Marxism, Leninism, Mao Zedong Thought; and the leadership of the Communist Party."

House-church leaders are not anti-Communist in socio-economic terms, but they do not believe that the Church should be used as a tool to control the political thinking of its members. Chinese Christians frequently quote Christ's words, "Render therefore to Caesar the things that are Caesar's, and to God the things that are God's" (Matt. 22:21, *RSV*).

6. *Discouragement of work among young people.* Christians opposed to the TSPM also point out that the government discourages all work among young people. Sunday Schools are not permitted. The Yunnan Document reiterates *Document 19* and states unequivocally: "It is forbidden to make converts among young people who are under age."[11] As has been noted, however, children from Christian homes are found in many churches.

The government has also made clear that it does not approve of infant baptism, and both Protestant and Roman Catholic churches have accepted this. So in that sense the government vetoes practices of which it does not approve, even to the extent of causing Christians to go contrary to long-accepted beliefs. A recently published "post-denominational catechism" suggests that baptisms be done indoors. Outside baptism would be contrary to the government policy of limiting religious activities to registered buildings. Some TSPM churches will not baptize anyone under 25, because that is the upper age limit for membership in the Communist Youth League. In some areas, 95 percent of the baptisms have been conducted in other than TSPM-related churches, which may indicate that young people find it easier to be baptized in the unregistered house churches.

The situation varies in many parts of the country. Many

young people have been baptized in the TSPM churches, and the youngest student at the Nanjing Seminary was only 17 when he enrolled.

7. *Church conformity to secular patterns.* The TSPM-related church has become an institution dependent on professional clergy. Further, it is controlled by local, provincial and national committees which set out rules and regulations for worship, for holding church office and for ways in which baptism and communion rites are to be administered. (Nonetheless, some variation is found among the churches.)

8. *Collaboration between church authorities and the PSB.* Christians opposed to joining the TSPM point to the constant collaboration between church authorities and the local PSB in tracking down evangelists and teachers who do not conform to TSPM regulations. Many Christians are very wary about what the government's future policy toward religion will be. Knowing that strong elements in the government believe that religion is evil and must be eventually rooted out of society, they fear that once all believers are compelled to join a government-controlled organization, it will be easier to enforce regulations to hinder church growth.

In all Communist countries there have been divisions between those prepared to accept government-sponsored organizations and those who, often at the cost of tremendous suffering, have maintained an independent witness. We who live outside China cannot influence the decision of those Christians residing within the country. *But whatever their decision, and whatever their organizational connection, we can support them in prayer.* We must, however, beware lest we make it more difficult for independent believers by giving undue recognition to an official body that may in time become the persecutor of those who do not join it.

If the Church is to fulfill God's purpose of proclaiming the gospel to all the peoples of China, it is essential that the Holy Spirit should control the appointment of leaders. Like the early apostles, they must be men and women who are filled with the Holy Spirit and who will speak the Word of God with boldness (see Acts 4:31).

We read that in the early church "the word of God increased; and the number of disciples multiplied greatly" (Acts 6:7). At the same time, the disciples "who were scattered went about preaching the word" (Acts 8:4) in spite of strong opposition. Christians in China ask for the same privilege. Will the Church humbly, and with love, maintain its vision to reach out to the 1 billion who have not heard the gospel? Or will it allow itself to be diluted in doctrine—confined and controlled by government regulations?

WHEN CAESAR IS HOSTILE

True followers of Christ often find themselves a despised minority. Their aims and values in life are rejected by the majority of those around whom they live. For the purpose of this book, we will define a hostile society as one that opposes Christian beliefs and values. To live in such a world is no new experience for Christians; first-century Christians regarded a hostile society as the *normal* environment for the disciple of Christ.

There are, of course, varying levels of hostility, or opposition. In some countries, hostility does not mean open persecution, but the atmosphere nevertheless is resistant to Christian witness. In many Western countries, technocratic capitalism is largely concerned with building the "kingdom of man," and as a result the Church in its midst faces subtle infiltration that tends to undermine Christian obedience to the truth of the gospel.

All who live in China today have to accept the Communist way of life. They usually have no choice as to where they live or the work they do. Ask young Chinese whether they like their jobs, and frequently they will start their reply by saying, "Our situation is quite different from yours in the West. We are not free to choose the work we would like to do."

Many of the questions that Chinese Christians are asking are different from the ones we would ask. It is not a relevant question for them whether or not they should go along with the Communist social system or their particular part in it. With regard to the system, they are, as one of them said, "like passengers on a train." The tracks have been laid, and they [the passengers] have no control over the direction in which the train is going. As Christians they love their country and can strive for the success of its socialist economic system. They do, however, have a responsibility to their "fellow passengers." And they are always conscious of the challenge to their faith by the Marxist world view.

Yet the nature of their responsibility to others changes from time to time. In a matter of a few years, the atmosphere can switch from virulent hatred of Christians to tolerance and respect for their integrity and contributions to society. But at any time, the winds of change may blow, and under the influence of another political campaign, their beliefs may once again become targets of attack. Thus, the intensity of the opposition alters from time to time and from place to place.

In order to appreciate what it means to be a disciple of Christ in China today, we must try to understand the nature of the problems faced by Chinese Christians. To a greater or lesser degree, the pressures described here apply to all Christian believers who are seeking to maintain a biblical faith in their life and world. That includes many who opted to attend TSPM churches when they reopened in 1979, as well as the independent house-church people.

Problems Faced By Chinese Christians Today

Rejection

At the beginning of the 1949 Revolution, Christians experienced a deep sense of rejection. Christianity was looked upon as a tool of imperialism, and Christians were regarded as followers of a foreign religion that supported the old regime.

Some of the early missionary pioneers like Hudson Taylor are still being attacked by political leaders in the TSPM. Church leaders recently attended a training session in which Hudson Taylor was declared to be an imperialist. A pastor from overseas who visited a class on Chinese Church history in Nanjing Theological Seminary reports that Hudson Taylor was described as:

> ... masquerading as a servant of God while actually representing colonial imperialistic foreign interests and having a materialistic interest in the vast coal and mineral deposits of China.[1]

Many Chinese were willing to suffer for the name of Christ, but it was much harder to be attacked because of their relationship with an American or British friend. Young Christians were prepared to give their allegiance to the new government and to take part in every constructive program that sought to build up the new China. Many Christian students joined teams that went out into the country to serve the peasants. They would even join in songs opposing American imperialism, but when it came to words of extravagant praise to Mao Zedong, including phrases like "our eternal liberator, we want no other savior," they faced a conflict of loyalties.

They were especially conscious of being rejected in their political discussion groups. Failure to accept the Marxist philosophy of life aroused the suspicion that they were reactionary in their thinking which put them in danger of being branded counterrevolutionary. Communist doctrine emphasizes a scientific and materialistic solution to all human problems, including poverty, selfish oppression and the inequalities of life. Like Christianity, it is a totalitarian philosophy, making demands on the whole of life. It [Communist doctrine] embraces every relationship.

Although dedicated Communists could be tolerant of religion in older people, believing it would soon die out, religious thought for the younger generation was an anathema. Not to accept the thinking of Marx, Lenin and Mao was taken as a sign that one's mind was still poisoned by imperialism, and such a person was therefore a hindrance to revolutionary progress. Younger Christians in particular found themselves a despised minority. They had what was called "bad class status." One Chinese Christian told me he had discovered what it means to be identified with the One who was "despised and rejected of men."

Is. 53

Political Discussion

In the early days of the Revolution, everyone had to spend many hours each week in compulsory indoctrination groups. After the fall of the Gang of Four these extremely unpopular political discussions were allowed to lapse or were made voluntary. When it became clear in the early 1980s that young people were losing faith in Marxism, weekly political groups were again made compulsory in universities and work units. Most students regarded these groups as the week's most boring lectures and some sought a way to avoid attending. A few dared to tell their teachers in one department that they were attending the political meetings in another department, and vice versa.

It is never easy for Christians to meet the barrage of criticism and questions that accompany political discussion sessions. Those who are not really grounded in the knowledge of Scripture may find it very hard to maintain their faith. To reject an atheistic, evolutionary philosophy inevitably provokes ridicule and causes Christians to be regarded as members of a superstitious minority who stand in the way of the development of the "glorious" Communist state. Such challenges have been especially hard on those with little opportunity for fellowship with other Christians.

Because of the lack of Christian literature, very few new believers have had opportunity to study books on Christian apologetics. In 1950 Christian students were greatly helped by a small book entitled *Questions Concerning the Faith*, published by the China Inter-Varsity Fellowship. It was the only Christian apologetic written by a Chinese under the Communist regime. Today it is very difficult to find such books in China.

Although it is true that Christians need to understand the arguments of dialectic materialism and "be ready always to give an answer for the hope that is in them" (see 1 Peter 3:15), the effectiveness of their witness depends more on the reality of their communion with God and the vitality of fellowship with other Christians, than on any other factors. Those who fail inevitably do so because they have lost touch with the source of their spiritual life.

Christian students in 1950 went through a five-week indoctrination course designed to change their thinking. During that time, the members of the fellowship met every evening to pray and discuss the problems they had faced during the day. They found they could not only answer many of the questions, but also could ask questions in return that the Communist students were incapable of answering. Their strategy proved so satisfactory that one non-Christian professor advised the students not to argue with Christians. "They are like a glass of water", he said. "If you leave it alone it remains calm and self-contained, but once you stir it up it spills and spreads all over the place."

The friend who shared that vignette with me went on to say, "Although we might answer a hundred of their questions, there would still be a hundred and one more problems waiting for a solution." Being able to answer particular questions is not the most important thing. Walking in close fellowship with God is what counts. If a child is walking in the dark with his father, someone may try to persuade him that since the father cannot be seen, he is not there. But the child knows better. His hand is firmly clasped in his father's. Doubts, if allowed to fester in the mind, may bring about loss of faith, but if brought into the light of fellowship with God and other Christians, doubts can be overcome. That is possible only when believers can be open with one another and are not afraid of being betrayed.

Thus, the great need for Christian witnessing in a Communist society is a support group of other Christians who trust each other and are fully loyal to Jesus Christ.

Self-criticism

Christians in China must always be ready to go through the self-criticism process. There is no freedom of silence in a Communist society. Attitudes must be openly expressed in discussion groups; books have even been published that outline how to write a self-criticism.

In the early days of the Revolution, students were required to write out again and again the story of their past experiences. They were under great pressure to confess wrong thinking, and were confronted with questions of truthfulness and honesty, both with regard to themselves and others. Even though "openness" was regarded as a virtue, they were constantly aware of the hypocrisy that characterized many of the confessions made by their friends. They knew that in order to survive in a Communist society, a person must say the "right" thing. One Christian girl was told by her friends that if she mentioned the fact that her parents formerly owned a hotel, she would be certain to get into trouble. She felt she must be honest, however, and so recorded that fact, even though she knew it could be used against her in the future.[2]

As recently as 1984, elementary school children were sometimes required to write self-criticisms. One small boy was asked to do this because he dropped to second place in his class.

In late 1983 a Christian college teacher was criticized publicly in his college and was later told to write a self-criticism because he had informed another colleague about where to attend a church service. These self-criticisms eventually end up in one's personal dossier and thus have long-term career implications.

Because the reports have to be constantly rewritten, great care must be taken not to contradict previous statements. Christians face the temptation to write declarations to please political leaders; they are under great pressure to profess enthusiasm for beliefs they inwardly reject. Some Christians have said that it is impossible to survive unless lip service is given to basic beliefs even when those beliefs contradict one's faith.

The question constantly arises as to what actually constitutes denial of the Saviour. In small group discussions they may be able to support current governmental policies in politics, social programs and economics, but when questions about God and human nature are presented, will they be able to speak the Christian truth boldly? It is not easy to be regarded as ideologically sick, needing to be liberated from past wrong thinking.

After the autobiographical report is written, it must be discussed with other study-group members. All members must undergo criticism by the group, and if Christians show no sign of changing their wrong thinking they were some times subjected to a "struggle session" in which they were at the center of attack.

Isolation

In the past, many Christians faced the problem of isolation from other believers. A beloved fellow worker whom I have known for over 30 years, gives a vivid picture of his experience during the 1950s.

Since I was regarded as obstinate in theology, I was transferred the day after my arrest to a single room for introspection. I was happy, for I could pray silently and repeat from memory the Word of God. I was deprived of the opportunity of any public manifestations of my faith, including giving thanks before meals. I tried to pray with my eyes open, but when the guard outside the window found I stopped for a while before I started to eat he questioned me severely and loudly: "What are you doing? Are you praying again?" Under such close surveillance, I had to give thanks when I saw the meals coming.

Being locked up resulted in self examination . . . I thought of my own life, my wife and my children . . . . When I was free outside, how easy it was for me to talk about "leaving wife or parents or children"! But then was not the time to carry it out. "Have I really left them for the sake of God?" The answer might often be negative. I realized my love of the world. Paul says in Gal. 6:14, "The world has been crucified to me, and I to the world." These two crucifixions are closely connected to each other. The first: "I have died to the world and no longer have any demand upon the world." The other: "The world has died to me and has no demands upon me." Only when you have died deeply and thoroughly can the world give up its demands on you.

My friend went on to describe how he discovered his own

weaknesses and sinfulness, and how he longed to attain the heights of spiritual life experienced by the apostle Paul. He was especially helped by the words, "Not to think of yourself more highly than you ought to think, but to think with sober judgment, according to the measure of faith God has assigned you" (see Romans 12:3).

After his period of solitary confinement he was put in a room that usually had more than 10 prisoners, sometimes 20 or 30.

> From morning till night the timetable was fully occupied except a short time before bed when I could pray. All day we were bombarded with the claim, "There is no God." Indeed it seemed that I was perplexed: "Where is God?" It reminded me of the sayings of Job 23:8-9, "Behold I go forward, but He is not there; and backward, but I cannot behold him." I had a little bit of Job's experience. However, I firmly believed in my God though I couldn't see Him, nor touch Him. Only a simple faith is the true faith . . . My faith was based on the rock. Because of this faith I was kept true and never denied the Lord's name. Our interrogator questioned me every two or three weeks: "How about your religious belief? What do you think of it now?" The only answer I gave him was to affirm that my belief was absolutely right.
>
> Finally he questioned me about Bible commentaries. I told him: "Bible commentaries were written by men; and men owing to their background, their education and the circumstances of their lives, may make some mistakes. But as far as the Bible itself is concerned, being inspired by God, it is absolutely right. I have complete faith in it."[3]

Many other Christians who were isolated from other believers found that because their time was so strictly regimented it was very hard to find any opportunity for quiet waiting upon God and for study of His Word. During the most severe times of testing, Christians did not dare to speak to one another. Any contact between them would be reported and would likely lead to prolonged questioning. For that reason, Christians avoided meeting one another on the street and did not visit each other's homes. For those sent to the countryside, re-education by labor kept them so busy that they had no time or solitude to think things through for themselves. They had to work until they were physically exhausted—whatever strength was left had to be used in political discussions.

Today most Christians no longer suffer the pressures experienced 10 years ago. Direct persecution is less common, but some Christians may find themselves tested by loneliness when they are sent to work in areas lacking Christian fellowship.

Family Pressures

The most severe testing for Christians has come through their own families. It was one thing for them to suffer themselves, but quite another for them to see their children suffer because of the parents' faith in Christ. A Christian couple during the Cultural Revolution was told, "You are deeply poisoned . . . but do not poison your children anymore." Because of the bad class status conferred on their parents, their children were mocked and insulted at school and often returned home crying.

One day the father was dragged out to be paraded through the streets, criticized and publicly denounced. Some who went through this experience never returned; others returned badly beaten. On this occasion the mother took the three children into the inner room and, shutting the door, they devoted themselves to prayer. The two older ones were in junior high school.

While the father was away, the mother told them the whole story of how he and many of his Christian friends had suffered because of their faith. She went on to say, "We are praying to God that our father may return to us safely. But God listens only to converted sinners, and our prayers will not come before God unless we have confessed our sins first." The children did confess their sins one by one with tears and sincerity, and all three were converted that day.

The father later described what happened to him:

While my family was praying for me at home, the officials gathered a large crowd to "struggle" against another man and me. Since I generally made no bad impression, the people's hatred could not be aroused against me, and they kept picking on the other man. After we were paraded through the streets with tall paper hats signifying our humiliation, when the gong was sounded we had to shout, "Down with so and so (our own names)!" I had no problem because I myself should have been overthrown long ago, [i.e., in the spiritual sense: "Not I, but Christ"]. I had been longing to be overthrown completely. Only when "self" is overthrown can Christ occupy the central position in our heart. Therefore I shouted loudly and the people approved . . . After being paraded through the streets, I was sent back home safely . . . When I got home and described to my family how the Lord had delivered me from the hands of men, they were overjoyed at the faithfulness of God and gave glory to Him. Seeing me back safely, the children were happy to know that God had indeed answered their prayer, and their faith in God was strengthened.

Later this couple's youngest son went through great personal testing. Although he did well in school, he was refused entry into senior high school because of the bad class status of his parents. It was terribly hard for this young man to see his fellow students going off to school while he was sent to work on the land. Later, however, God opened a way for him to go not only to high school, but also to college.

Some Christian families suffered because the children were taught in school to report anything suspicious or reactionary about their parents. For example, during the Cultural Revolution, a couple who regularly prayed, read the Bible and sang hymns at home found that all three of their daughters had joined the Red Guards. The girls constantly taunted their parents: "Stop praying, stop reading those books and singing those hymns, or we will report you." Undaunted, the couple replied, "If you wish to do that, go right ahead. We are not afraid. We fear God and will follow Him only." One daughter subsequently joined the Communist Party, but upon her father's death, she came to true faith in God.

Betrayal

In 1950, when Ruth and I were still in China, we heard of some Christians who denied their Lord. Their testimonies were published and made the subject of much discussion. That caused great agony for those who sought to remain true to the faith. Christians frequently found themselves attacked by others, and sometimes by those who formerly had confessed faith in Christ.

It is not the worst thing to suffer at the hands of nonbelievers, but it is terribly hard to be criticized by fellow Christians. Clearly, believers ought neither to deny the Lord nor to betray one another, but during the intense suffering of the Cultural Revolution, many whose love for Christ was very real failed to live up to those principles. Today, Christians recall brothers and sisters who "betrayed the Lord and betrayed their friends." Not all who did that were "wolves in sheep's clothing." Some of them bitterly regretted what they had done. Like Christ, Christians today have to learn to forgive those who under great pressure become weak and fail.

Lost Job Opportunities

Another danger that Christians have faced is the relentless urging that they should give up their faith in order to get a good job. Young people especially seem to find it hard to resist such pressure. One Christian was reminded constantly that he had no future unless he turned away from his faith. In the beginning, he felt he should continue working in the fields as an ordinary laborer and maintain a Christian witness there. But later, as the pressure continued, the day came when he agreed to turn away from his faith and accept a better job. He received letters from his home and church, but did not respond. Later, his father and uncle went to see him, bringing pictures of the Christian group back home, but he rejected their pleas to come back to faith in Christ. Then the two older men were both arrested, paraded through the streets and ridiculed by the young people of the town. Such a travesty spoke to the young man's heart. As he saw the grace and patience with which his father and uncle bore that suffering, he was won back to Christ.

Young people from Christian families face a great trial of faith when they are invited to join the Communist Youth League, since membership affects the kind of job they receive after graduation. One Christian university student was the pride of the English department. Everyone praised her good work but did not know its source; she kept her Christian faith a secret. She was, however, the only one in her department neither from the Party nor the Communist Youth League. She was urged to join the League in order to make the whole class "a sheet of red," but she made an excuse not to. As a result, a "help" meeting was called and at that meeting, feeling she could no longer hide her faith, she plainly stated, "I am a Christian."

> I couldn't believe what happened next! Suddenly the meeting turned into an occasion to "eradicate feudal superstition." And here was a living negative example to give all the workers assembled there a lesson in thought struggle!

She closed her eyes to pray for help, then told the whole assembly, more than 200 students and teachers, about Christ's suffering for the world, and that Christians could not harm society.

> When I finished what I had to say, the leader of the Workers' Propaganda Team looked as if he suddenly woke up from a dream. He immediately upbraided me for using the university as a platform to spread my "poison," and he wanted everyone to bring out their criticisms. But the people had already felt the goodness of God; they did not use the standard critical words . . . Unhappy, the leaders dispersed the criticism meeting.

The young woman was sure she would now have to leave school, and was ready to face what developed.

> The university was very important to me, but compared to God, it was not worth speaking about. The grace of God demands that we put aside ourselves. I can give up many things, but I cannot give up God.

Some ridiculed her. Others were sympathetic, and still others came privately to ask about salvation. Several meetings were held to decide whether she would be expelled.

> The school definitely wanted to keep me; the Workers' Propaganda Team thought I was a "reactionary," and had to be expelled. Finally they reached a compromise; expulsion from the school would depend on the investigation by the school. But when assignment came after graduation, they said, I would have to be assigned to a rural village.

She rejoiced nonetheless, and for the remainder of her student days shared the gospel with many other students. "I did not want merely to be at the university, but I wanted the gospel to be spread widely from here."[4]

Christian Integrity Tested

Christians are constantly faced with the temptation to compromise their integrity. In a Communist society, truth is always relative. In politics, people endeavor to say the right thing whether or not it is true. Communism seeks to control all thinking, but Communist policy is always changing. In order to gain favor with the Party, people have to keep up with current thought patterns and follow current political slogans.

During the Cultural Revolution everyone had to support Mao's policy of common ownership of land, with no private plots. At that time, Liu Shaoqi, who had more or less been running the country, was denounced as a terrible villain and "capitalist roader." But a decade later Mao's policy was reversed and Liu Shaoqi rehabilitated, so that those who seemingly supported Mao Thought enthusiastically during the Cultural Revolution were now saying the opposite.

If there should be another change in policy, political discussion groups across the country would be required to follow the new slogans. If the CCP says that something is black, everybody must agree that it is black; if a few months later they say it is white, everyone must acknowledge that it is white. How can Christians maintain their personal integrity and at the same time go along with such reversals?

Telling lies to benefit one's self is no less common in China than in any Western country. And sometimes Christians are tempted too. But the temptation to lie is even greater in a society where telling the truth can have dangerous consequences for the individuals involved.

For example, a friend of mine who led a small Christian house group loaned a listening tape to a Christian sister. She in turn, without his permission, loaned it to someone else. That person played it loud enough for his neighbors to hear, and they reported him to the police. Questioned about its source, he gave the name of the Christian woman and let her know that she, too, might be interrogated.

Scared, and not wanting to expose the house-group leader, she went to my friend and asked if it would be all right to say she'd gotten it along with some other tapes from Indonesia. He said no; she must speak the truth, whatever the consequences to him. He was a man who already had undergone great persecution, including imprisonment. To the relief of everyone, the woman was never questioned.

Bribery

Today in China, as in many other countries, it is very difficult to obtain anything without giving special gifts in return. CCP members have great power to bestow privileges, get good jobs and obtain other material benefits. When a request is made to them, they often say they will consider it, which frequently means they are waiting to see what will be given to them. Christians too are frequently tempted by the opportunity to gain advantages for themselves by giving gifts to friends in the Party.

A related question is deciding to what extent Christians can rightfully take advantage of the common practice of "going through the back door." For instance, a person who has a doctor friend can get special medicines and perhaps even preferential treatment. The doctor, in turn, knows that the one coming to him also has certain privileges and may be able to reciprocate in some way. Further complications result when the doctor's friend is approached by another person who wants special medicines and so asks for an introduction to the doctor.

In China, so much depends on relationships. This practice, of course, is not new. It was prevalent in imperial times and is common in many countries where goods are scarce and a privileged class can bestow favors.

False Reports

Another common practice is to prepare false reports about the production of a work unit, which then are used to obtain extra benefits. The profits that accrue as a result of these false reports are then divided among unit members. If a Christian in the unit refuses to go along, he could find himself in serious trouble.

One Christian woman kept accounts for a dining hall. The Communist officials trusted her and were glad to have her honest accounting, but later one of them wanted to gain some privilege for himself and asked her to prepare a false account. She refused. For a long time, great pressure was brought to bear on her, but she would not give in. Finally, the harassment was so upsetting to her that she broke down mentally and had to be sent to a psychiatric hospital.

Attitude to the Communist Party

Christians are often watched in order to see if their political attitude is right. Even today students are required to write regular assessments of how their political thinking has progressed. One Christian engineering student facing this dilemma described how difficult it was to write these papers—since in the Lord Jesus Christ she had found a true freedom and hope that she had not found in Marxist-Leninist thought.

The Communist system requires that everybody be active in the highly-structured Communist network, supporting it in every possible way. From time to time, meetings are held in which participants may be asked to reveal their attitude toward current policies. This includes questions as to whether they have been honest in the confession of past wrong thinking. They still may also be required to report on others. The unit committee will watch to see if they are really active in the work and thinking process of the local organization. If they show themselves politically alert and supportive of the Party, they are accepted and encouraged. But often in order to gain a position of acceptance with the Party they must betray others—so that anyone who gets to the top tends to climb on the backs of others to get there. Those who keep apart from the Party and avoid political discussions are frequently suspected of harboring counterrevolutionary thoughts.

One Christian, after becoming the deputy head of his factory, often found himself meeting with other factory heads and their deputies, all of whom were Party members. He was praised by them and offered special privileges, in an effort to get him to join the CCP. For several years he refused, and finally was demoted and sent to another factory. If he had given in and denied his faith, he would most likely have obtained an important position.

Undoubtedly, there are many secret believers in the Party and Communist Youth League, but if it is discovered that they are Christians they are ordered to renounce their faith. If they refuse, they can be expelled from the organization.

Concerning Marriage

Christians in China face the problem of finding life partners who share their faith. There are fewer Christian men than women, and some men marry non-Christian brides, so it is often very difficult for a Christian woman to find a Christian man to marry. As already noted, Communist policy strongly opposes any teaching that would encourage believers to marry only within the faith. In spite of such difficulties, however, many Christians can testify to remarkable guidance in this matter.

Confession of Faith

Especially among intellectuals, many Christians are not willing to let their colleagues and friends know that they are Christians. Rather, they keep their faith private and meet secretly in their homes. One Christian professor told me he knew the biblical teaching about confessing Christ before men, but felt it was impossible for him to do so. His whole family would suffer if he was dismissed from his position because of professing his faith to others.

A scientist who recently became a Christian in America said he was sure that if he went back to his homeland and admitted he was a Christian, he would lose his position. Everyone would know that his dismissal was because of that, and then others would be afraid to follow Christ.

It is easy to point to the teaching of Scripture and the example of innumerable others who have suffered throughout the centuries because of their faith. Yet we who have never experienced life in a Communist society are in no position to criticize those who face such difficult tests of faith.

Some would not agree that Christians in China are still living in a hostile society. Political leaders in religious organizations emphasize the help that the government has given to the churches; they deny the existence of persecution except during the Cultural Revolution. Often they insist that a Christian who is truly patriotic and supports the socialist state, accepting the leadership of the CCP, has nothing to fear. But that often means that Christians must limit their witness to their immediate circle of family and friends, making no effort to reach out to the unevangelized.

Among their non-Christian neighbors, Christians may have many good friends and a reputation for loving service in the community. But in their secular work they often face criticism from members of their unit. If their faith is known to Party officials, they will be regarded with suspicion—in any future political campaign Christians may well again be targets of attack.

Christians are less likely to face difficulties if they make no attempt to share their faith with others. It is those who actively participate in the mission of the Church, speaking the gospel to those who do not know Christ, who will be most conscious of the spiritual warfare.

CHINA AND THE CHURCH
WORLDWIDE

Chinese Christians were shut off from the Church outside China for almost 30 years. Ignorance of what was happening to believers inside China meant that Christians in other countries could neither share in the suffering of their brothers and sisters nor learn from their experiences. Now that the door has been opened for limited communication, members of the global Church are asking how a meaningful fellowship with Chinese Christians can be developed. It is not a question of what we can do for them, but rather what we can learn from their experience, and minister to them, as they also minister to us.

Before considering the best ways to relate to Christians in China, however, let us first note four characteristics that should be evident in our own lives.

1. *We need a spirit of thanksgiving.*

We must be thankful for the church growth that has taken place in China. In spite of sealed borders during the Cultural Revolution, and the ban on all missionary work or assistance from outside, the number of Christians has increased much more rapidly than in countries where missionaries have been permitted to work. Intense persecution and suffering experienced by almost all Christians have resulted in revival, rather than in dissolution. In contrast, it is often true that in lands where there has been affluence and toleration Christian growth has been slow, and much Christian witness has lacked the vitality necessary for healthy growth.

We do not suggest that the Church in China has come through its suffering unscathed; a spirit of human "triumphalism" would be inappropriate. Just as we are aware of great failures in our own Christian communities, we are aware of weakness in the Church in China. But we can give deep thanks for what God has done there.

2. *We need a spirit of confession.*

When all missionaries left China, the West was sometimes guilty of unbelieving pessimism. Seeing a weak and divided Church, we felt we had failed. We knew many dedicated men and women and outstanding spiritual leaders. But could they, a tiny minority, stand against the mighty tide of a triumphant Communist ideology that proclaimed the "kingdom of man"—with no place for a crucified Saviour?

With no news of those we loved, our prayers became general and sporadic; most of us failed to enter into a continuous persevering prayer of faith. Now, as we hear of faithful witness in the midst of trial and great poverty, we feel rebuked for our lethargy, easy-going ways, affluence and lack of concern for the poor. The example set by the witness of the Chinese Church calls us to examine our own life-style and dedication.

3. *We need a spirit of humility.*

We cannot think of going back to China as "missionaries from a superior Western civilization." We know that many of the early pioneer missionaries showed deep and humble appreciation of China's culture and longevity. At the same time, many spoke from positions of power. Even in the twentieth century, missionaries represented the wealthy West. They introduced modern education and technology and dispensed relief to an impoverished, war-torn nation that had been humiliated by Western nations.

Many missionaries did not realize they had that kind of image. Often they lived sacrificial lives as close as possible to the people, and were regarded with real affection by them. Nonetheless, the young nationalists of China viewed the large mission schools and compounds in the cities as institutions of cultural imperialism.

If the door to missionaries had opened, when church doors

opened in 1979, it might well have led to an influx of competing Western organizations bringing in their denominations and all kinds of equipment and methodology. Once again, an image of power and superiority might have been created.

If we believe that our sovereign God overruled in allowing both the overthrow of the Gang of Four and the introduction of a more liberal policy toward religion, then surely we can also believe that it was in His purpose that missionaries were not allowed to return, and that the responsibility for evangelism remained with the Chinese Church.

A Chinese Christian once remarked, "In the past we blew trumpets and had large evangelistic campaigns. Some believed, but not great numbers. Now we have very little equipment; the message has to be spread by quiet prayerful sharing of the gospel by individuals with family and neighbors—and many are coming to the Lord."

Perhaps in the future the Lord will again allow some of His servants from the West to participate with Chinese Christians, at their invitation, in making the gospel known to the millions who have not yet heard. "And this gospel of the kingdom shall be preached in all the world for a witness unto all nations; and then shall the end come" (Matt. 24:14, *KJV*). That witness, the task of the worldwide Church, requires Christians of all races to work together. In China today, missionaries are not welcomed. But the door is open for individuals from other countries to serve the Chinese people as engineers, doctors, business people, teachers and students. In this way, it is possible for servants of Christ coming from the outside to be part of the Christian presence in China.

To have a humble attitude means that we cannot afford to be judgmental. There are still many things that people living outside China cannot understand. Chinese Christians, too, have different viewpoints. We must hold fast to scriptural principles, while recognizing that the way in which those principles are applied in China must be decided by Chinese Christians. We are called to pray for all who meet in the name of our Lord and who truly manifest the life of Christ, whatever their particular organizational affiliation. And we should especially remember those who are still suffering because of their faith.

4. *We need an understanding of history.*

We should not just be stirred emotionally by reports from the Chinese Church. Our emotional response must be influenced by our theological convictions and the lessons we have learned from Church history. Under the Roman empire, in the pre-Constantine era, Christians were regarded with suspicion. The Church was frequently treated as an illegal organization. After Constantine, the Church was given official status and too often was used by the state for political gain. From time to time, groups of Christians, disturbed by this misuse of the Church and the decline of spiritual life, would withdraw from the state Church and seek revival, even though that stance frequently brought persecution.

The situation in China is, of course, different from the situation both before and after Constantine. Christianity is no longer regarded as an illegal religion, although it is still considered detrimental to the development of true Communist society. In assessing the present situation, we must understand the past history of the Church in China and think through the implications and possible long-term results of present governmental policies.

Our understanding of the Church today cannot be based on reports of large crowds attending certain TSPM churches. Far more important is the continuing freedom to develop a vibrant loving community experiencing the purifying work of the Holy Spirit, directed by leaders "approved by God to be entrusted with the gospel, [speaking] not to please men but to please God who tests our hearts" (1 Thess. 2:4). Only as our vision of God's purpose for the Church is clear can we avoid the danger of a superficial view of the religious situation in China.

How Christians Outside China Can Help

Broadcasting

Christian broadcasting is perhaps one of the most important ways for Christians to introduce the gospel of Jesus Christ to those inside China. During the Cultural Revolution, when no public teaching or preaching was possible, the only source of Christian encouragement for many believers was the radio programs from the Far East Broadcasting Company (FEBC). Even though the FEBC received only a very few letters in response each year (see map), they continued to broadcast— believing that the message was reaching many in China. Listening to what was considered to be an "enemy" radio station was forbidden at that time, but numbers of Christians and often other young people would listen secretly at night, with their receivers hidden under their bed rolls. Christians were encouraged and unbelievers were converted.

In 1979 the category of "enemy stations" was removed from a number of Western stations, e.g., BBC, Voice of America, and Voice of Friendship (FEBC). Thousands of letters were received by Christian broadcasting stations as a result. Those letters provided overwhelming evidence of what Christian radio broadcasting had meant to vast numbers of people. Many wrote saying they became Christians through listening to the message. Because of the dearth of Bible teachers and Christian literature, new Christians especially were glad to be encouraged in their faith through radio teaching.

Apart from the testimonies in letters, reports from Chinese churches also indicate the important role of broadcasting. A pastor in one TSPM church told me about a young man who visited his church looking for a Bible. It was his first visit to a church and he told my friend that he was the first pastor he had ever met. He got up in the church service and told how he had become a Christian through listening to the radio—but as soon as he finished speaking, another of the TSPM pastors came up to him and asked him never to mention the radio again. TSPM officials, unlike the masses of people who attend the churches, are opposed to all Christian broadcasting. Notices have even sometimes been posted, warning Christians not to listen.

The reasons given for this opposition are: (1) Christian broadcasting from outside is a form of cultural imperialism; (2) it violates the Three-Self principles, since the content is not

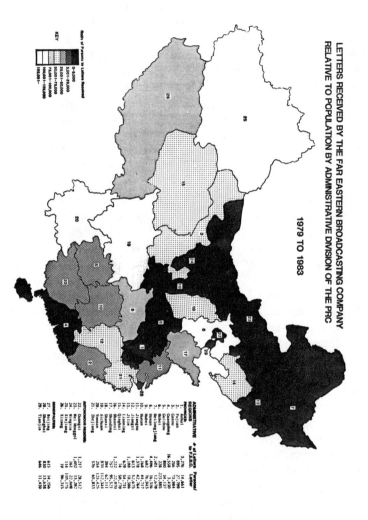

Far Eastern Broadcasting Company,
Encyclopedia of China Today (1981)

controlled by the TSPM; and (3) some of the programs are very Western and therefore unsuitable.

The TSPM regards Christian broadcasting as an attempt by the outside Church to interfere. TSPM spokespersons say that through this activity Chinese Christians are made dependent on foreign help; they are encouraged to maintain links with Western organizations considered unfriendly to the TSPM.

The millions of Christians in China who have benefited from the Christian broadcasts might reply that the Church throughout the world is one, and they should not be afraid of accepting some help from outside Christians—especially since no officially-organized Christian broadcasting is allowed inside China.

With the growth in the number of Christians, the existing resources for teaching are inadequate. In that gap, the radio can provide effective teaching for those who have no access to Christian teachers and literature. It can also bring the gospel to the homes of people who might never enter a church building.

Today, many of the radio programs are prepared by Chinese Christians whose ministry can hardly be described as "cultural imperialism." It is true that some programs may be too Westernized in character, but listeners are obviously free to choose which programs they will listen to.

To many it appears that TSPM opposition is a form of censorship and must stem from its desire to control the Church in China, as well as cooperate with the government in limiting the spread of the gospel. It has been suggested that some TSPM leaders personally may not oppose Christian radio broadcasting. They must, however, oppose it in public because they know of the government's dislike for the wide dissemination of the gospel by means of radio. But they could never admit that this was the reason for their opposition.

As noted earlier, one TSPM spokesman has stated that they are not interested in seeing great numbers turn to Christ, since they do not have sufficient resources to care for a lot of untaught Christians.[1] Yet that viewpoint does not take into account the work of the Holy Spirit. If God is causing men and women to seek Christ, He is able to provide means of nurturing them in the faith. Radio broadcasting is one of those means.

While we can understand the desire for the Chinese Church not to be dependent on foreign sources, it is hard to understand an attitude that puts nationalism above the purpose of God. We know that "[He] desires all men to be saved and to come to the knowledge of the truth" (1 Tim. 2:4). Programs designed especially to train Christian workers are broadcast so that many more leaders may be raised up in the Chinese Church who "rightly handle the word of truth" (see 2 Tim. 2:15).

Few people realize the cost of an effective broadcasting ministry. In addition to high financial expenses (connected with equipment and the rising cost of electricity), there is the constant need for dedicated and qualified personnel. To maintain many hours of broadcasting everyday requires a large staff of engineers and programmers.

Perhaps the greatest need is for script writers who know the Scriptures and understand Chinese thought patterns. Truth is changeless, but it needs to be expressed in cultural terms that can be understood by listeners. Among the large number of gifted Chinese students and graduates studying and teaching in Western universities, there surely should be some who will hear the call of God to this strategic radio ministry.

Literature

For many years Chinese Christians were almost completely deprived of Bibles and books that could build up their faith. It is hard for us to realize how seriously our churches would be affected if they had to work without any Christian literature. So much of what we know about Christ and His claims, demands and promises has come from the reading of His Word and other books.

Without Christian literature, the Church becomes spiritually impoverished. So it is not surprising that, when communications were again opened with China, the great cry was for Bibles and literature. For a short time, visitors were free to take in small amounts of Christian literature, and Bibles could be sent in by mail. Gradually, however, restrictions were once again tightened.

We can understand the government's opposition to large-scale smuggling operations, but it is not accurate to use the word *smuggling* in relation to the Bible. Since 1979 the Bible has not been regarded as illegal, and therefore it cannot be considered smuggling for a Christian visitor to take in a few Bibles. Suitcases are subject to inspection, although usually they are not opened. In any case, if Bibles are found, and objected to, they must then be surrendered to officials.

Bibles and Christian books are so urgently needed that Chinese Christians go to great lengths to obtain them. Because Bibles printed in China use the old script, young people—accustomed to the new abbreviated characters—find them difficult to read. So we rejoice in all the books that have been safely delivered to eagerly-awaiting Chinese believers.

We must realize, however, that Christians in China who receive Bibles and literature from the outside face considerable risk, since the government, assisted by the TSPM, is determined to prevent the free flow of such materials throughout China. On one occasion, a TSPM pastor begged me not to attempt to bring Bibles in, saying the government fears that great quantities of Bibles might be made available to the general population.

That, of course, is not the reason given publicly by the TSPM. Their reasons are the same as those relating to broadcasting. They have already printed more than 1 million Bibles or New Testaments, and although they recognize that people are still without Bibles, they urge Christians to wait until more are printed inside the country, rather than looking to outside sources. The same arguments are used against receiving Bible-study materials and devotional literature. Chinese Christians are constantly told they must not receive religious literature from the outside.

If a Bible printed in China is legal, why should an identical Bible printed in Hong Kong be regarded as subversive? While acknowledging their inability to provide adequate supplies of teaching material, the TSPM still opposes entry from the outside. The only exception has been the acceptance of books for TSPM seminary libraries officially received as gifts and, occasionally, small quantities of literature for their pastors. At that, only books authorized by the TSPM can be received.

On one occasion when I took some Chinese commentaries and booklets to a church, I was asked not to give any to church members but to leave everything with the pastors. Later I heard of a church where one whole floor of the building was filled with Bibles brought in by tourists, gathering dust. Ironically, there is no objection to bringing in all kinds of Western scientific textbooks, but even the most standard Christian classics are not wanted.

Publishing and distribution are not the only problem. The Church in China needs writers, men and women who are able to express the faith in ways their people can understand. Young intellectuals, dissatisfied with Marxism, need a Christian apologetic. Christians struggling with issues of church and state relationships need a thoughtful presentation of biblical principles written by their own people.

A writing program needs to be developed, and Chinese Christians, as well as Chinese theologians living in the West, need to be encouraged to face the challenge of presenting the gospel to intellectuals. Others must consider creative ways of explaining the message of Christ to the millions of country people with low levels of education.

A number of Chinese Christian organizations in Hong Kong have produced booklets, tracts and hymnbooks especially suited for the Church in China. The Christian Communications Ltd. (CCL) has published and distributed mini-libraries: Bible commentaries, dictionaries, concordances, handbooks, devotional books and other Bible study materials. These valuable libraries have been delivered to hundreds of pastors and house-church leaders and are greatly sought after by Christians, even though they are aware of the danger of being found with literature from outside the country.

Chinese Scholars

Throughout Chinese history, highly-skilled Chinese have gone overseas to study and after their return have had a significant impact on their country. After the period of rejection during the Cultural Revolution, Chinese scholars again have taken leadership roles. They are still like mustard seeds being planted, but someday they may become great trees that will form the foundation of modernized Chinese society.

Thousands of Chinese scholars are coming to Western nations and to Japan. During their time overseas they enjoy freedom from many of the restraints they face at home. But when they first arrive they experience culture shock. Sometimes they are appalled by the lax moral standards of Western societies. They greatly need friends who will interpret for them the new thought patterns and standards of life in their host country. In many places, they have met Christians—Western scientists and teachers, fellow students and Christian families—who have regarded them not as targets for evangelism, but as friends from whom much can be learned. Their new friends do not pressure these Chinese scholars to become Christians, but rather wait for them to ask questions before talking about their faith. They open their homes and show them the love of Christ. Some have taken them on tours during school vacations or have invited them to Christmas functions.

One Chinese scholar told me he had come to Canada prejudiced against Christianity, but found that all of his new friends were Christians. "They are such excellent people," he said, "and my whole attitude to Christianity has changed." Another Chinese student commented, "I find that the people who are really reliable are those I meet in church."

Since they have been told to study the culture of their host country, Chinese scholars are often willing to visit churches. Sometimes, however, they hesitate to accept an invitation if they feel they may be criticized by their Chinese colleagues. An American Christian professor invited three Chinese scholars to church and they kept postponing their visit. Finally, one of them told the professor that two of them wanted to go but they were not sure about the third. If he did not go and they did, he might report them to the Chinese authorities.

In England and North America, Chinese students are seeing the reality of Christian faith in the lives of their friends. Some have found new life in Christ and returned to witness to their families. Many more have gone back with a very favorable attitude to Christianity. Sadly, however, many never have the opportunity of entering a Christian home.

Thousands more will come in the next few years. If Christians are faithful in giving their time and friendship, seeds may be planted in Chinese society that will bear much fruit in the future.

Christians Serving in China

China's Four Modernizations policy calls for large numbers of "foreign experts." It also opens the door for foreign students to study in China. Joint projects between China and Western countries mean increased opportunities for Christians to enter China. Not only teachers of English, but also medical doctors and people with higher degrees in many different disciplines, are needed. More openings exist than can be filled, and Christians need to recognize this "open door." Dedicated and qualified people are not easy to find.

In the early months of 1985, as this book is being completed, China's economic growth is so evident and so many changes are taking place that there is considerable optimism. Many people believe that as business and cultural contacts with the West multiply, so will there be increasing freedom for Christians in professional positions to be a part of the witness of the Church in China.

Some of the organizations recruiting teachers for China are known to be Christian and have entered into contracts with various government departments and academic institutions. Their work has been much appreciated because of the quality of their teaching and the helpful attitude of their teachers. Their service has been in the secular field, with no connection between them and the TSPM.

Changes are taking place, however. On March 22, 1985 it was announced in Hong Kong that Bishop Ding would be invited to serve as president of the Amity Foundation, a newly-formed organization for the purpose of "promoting health, education and social service projects in the People's Republic of China." The

Foundation welcomes funds from overseas to be used in projects such as the Children's Mental Health Research Center and for the "recruiting of foreign teachers from church agencies for service in Chinese institutes of higher learning which do not normally have foreign teachers." Bishop Ding described the Amity Foundation as a People's Organization sponsored by Chinese Christians and Chinese citizens. It will be registered by the government as an independent organization separate from the TSPM and CCC.

While insisting that there is no change in the Three-Self principles, it does indicate that TSPM is seeking financial support from "friendly" foreign Christian organizations, with a view to contributing toward China's modernization. It will also seek to influence the appointment of English teachers and is asking churches overseas to keep TSPM informed about the activities of Christians teaching in China.[2]

The policy of not allowing missionaries to work as missionaries in China remains unchanged. But increasing numbers of Christians are finding opportunity there through secular positions. They cannot engage in active evangelism, but they can reveal the true meaning of the Christian life through the quality of their lives, the professionalism of their work and their ability to make friends.

Being under constant observation, often isolated from other Christians, bewildered by culture shock and frustrated with the difficulties of understanding how the Chinese authorities work can all lead to discouragement and depression. Yet the majority of those who go to China will find the difficulties are far outweighed by the joys of serving eager students and of establishing friendships with spiritually hungry people.

Many have returned home from service in China with a deep love for the Chinese people. It is a privilege to share not only the gospel but also one's own self (see 1 Thess. 2:8).

Overseas Chinese Visitors

Many Chinese Christians in the West, with relatives in China, now have a wonderful opportunity to visit their homeland

and share their faith with them. The Chinese government extends a warm welcome to overseas Chinese, especially to those who may make some contribution to the Four Modernizations program. Many Chinese scientists and medical doctors have been invited to give lectures. If they are Christians it is important for them to make their faith known so as to emphasize the fact that those with high academic qualifications believe in and experience the reality of Christ.

Chinese visitors can go to places closed to Western tourists. Returning to the villages and small towns of their relatives, they are able to get a much more realistic view of life in that area than members of tour groups. Chinese born in the affluent society of the West will experience a measure of culture shock when they see the very simple life-style of their relatives whose annual income would not be sufficient for one month's expenses in the West. They will receive a warm welcome from friends who are eager to receive news of the outside world. Some relatives will hear the gospel for the first time from their guests, enjoy Christian fellowship and receive valuable teaching materials. The Chinese visitor, in turn, may learn new lessons in faith and come away with a fresh vision of the need in China.

Prayer

Requests that we should pray for the Church in China are very familiar, and it is easy to assent to the importance of prayer. Yet it is much more difficult actually to engage in disciplined, Spirit-guided and effective intercession. True prayer requires both a recognition of the presence of God and an identification with the people for whom we are praying. The love of God shed abroad in our hearts flows out from us to those for whom we pray.

From the biblical example of Daniel we see that prayer involves spiritual conflict. Daniel was concerned that the Kingdom of God be revealed to the secular rulers of his day. He was prepared to serve in the court of the king of Babylon, but he refused any compromise that would interfere with his unique witness to the one true God. (One Chinese Christian doctor wrote, "I believe that Daniel's prayer was more important than his witness, because without prayer his witness would have been impossible.")

Daniel saw prayer as a priority and continued to pray three times every day, even when he knew it could cost him his life. In addition to those times, there were periods when he gave himself to special intercession for his people. He was convinced that God had a purpose for Israel and would be glorified through the people who bore the Lord's name. From his study of God's Word through Jeremiah, he became certain that the time had come for God to deliver His people.

His prayer (recorded in Daniel 9) illustrates how a person can identify with those who are in the midst of trouble. From the response to this prayer we can also see that there is a parallel between the political developments and conflicts on earth, and the conflict in heavenly places. Daniel was engaged in spiritual warfare and was described as a man "greatly beloved," whose prayers not only were heard but also resulted in action being taken (see Dan. 10:12-14). The intensity of his prayer challenges us to engage in this kind of prayer ourselves for the people in China who "are called by the name of the Lord."

In Paul's prayer for the persecuted church in Thessalonica we see the same kind of earnestness:

> "Night and day we pray most earnestly that we may see you again and supply what is lacking in your faith . . . . May the Lord make your love increase and overflow for each other and for everyone else, just as ours does for you. May he strengthen your hearts so that you will be blameless and holy in the presence of our God and Father when our Lord Jesus comes with all his holy ones" (1 Thess. 3:10,12-13, *NIV*).

Paul's concern was not just for the Thessalonians' conversion but for the continuous working of the Spirit in their lives until the day of Christ's appearing.

Like Paul, we need to have discernment as we pray. What kind of Church is God seeking to build in China? What is He wanting to accomplish in His Church? Where are the hidden enemies? What are the greatest needs? Can we see the course of the spiritual battle and take our stand alongside faithful servants of Christ, striving that every man and woman may be presented perfect in Christ?

Paul prayed in a similar way for those whom he had never seen. "I want you to know how much I am struggling for you and for those at Laodicea and for all who have not met me personally" (Col. 2:1, *NIV*).

It is not easy to pray for those whom we have never met, but we can do a number of things to help make our intercession more meaningful.

For example, we can:

1. Read as much as possible about China, especially about the Chinese Church (see Bibliography).

2. Join a prayer fellowship that provides specific daily requests for prayer for China, and keep it with your Bible so that you can pray regularly (see Resources).

3. Join a local prayer group that is praying for China, or start one yourself. The dynamics of several people joining together can be an aid to intercessory prayer.

4. Get to know people from China. There may be some in your own neighborhood who have recently come from the mainland. You may even meet Chinese Christians who can give you valuable information and help you understand the needs of Christian families in China.

5. Talk to friends who have been living and working in China, asking them to share their insights into the nature of modern Chinese society.

As we study the situation in China and pray for our Chinese brothers and sisters, the more we will realize that "a people for His name" is being called out in China. The revival that has begun could very well sweep across the entire continent. China could yet become a "light" to the nations of the East.

Afterword

As I finish this book, I see before me many different representatives of the Church in China. There is a respected retired professor from a background of several generations of Christians, who accompanies Christian doctors from the West on lecture tours requested by Chinese medical authorities; there is a former fellow worker, now confined through illness to her home, whose prayer life and loving concern are an inspiration to all who visit her. On a bulletin board by my desk I see a picture of a friend who worked among students. He sent me a photograph of his ordination and now rejoices that he can again preach the gospel and lead a Bible study which is attended by 100 people. Another picture shows the wife of a Chinese Christian, now overseas, who meets with friends and neighbors who come to her for Bible teaching; some have come to know Christ in her home.

There are other pictures of doctors and scientists who excel in various fields of research and medical practice and thus commend the gospel of Christ by the quality of their lives. One of them recently told me about meeting a Christian farmer on the train who spends his time traveling from village to village ministering to believers, some of them barely literate and urgently needing biblical training. One young man engaged in rural evangelism described to me the dangers accompanying that kind of work.

In addition to Christians in China, I also see the Church in

Hong Kong seeking to prepare for the changes that will take place in 1997 when China resumes sovereignty over that crowded territory. A revived Christian community in Hong Kong could play an important part in reaching out to the Mainland.

These few I have mentioned represent millions of Christians who make up the Body of Christ in China. As members of the Kingdom of God, their lives bear witness to the mission of Christ "to preach good news to the poor, to proclaim release to the captive, and recovery of sight to the blind, to set at liberty those who are oppressed" (see Luke 4:18). We rejoice that through them God is fulfilling His purpose of love for the people of China. For them and for us, the long march of the Church will end in that great day when the cry goes forth, "The kingdom of the world has become the kingdom of our Lord and of His Christ and He will reign for ever and ever" (see Rev. 11:15).

Appendices

Appendix 1

TSPM Document on Church Reorganization and Practice in the City of Taiyuan

All the pastors of every [Protestant] Christian Church in Taiyuan, after undergoing socialist education studies and handing their hearts over to the Party, feel deeply that the old ways of running the Church, and the economic and personal structures left by the imperialist missionaries, are not suited to the socialist system of our 600 million people and must be changed:

The whole city will set up unified worship, with a ministerial staff of three or four. All ministerial staff apart from those left in the church and in the work of the patriotic committee will take part in socialist construction:

1. In regard to organizational structures, all the original committees of each church will be terminated and the administration of church affairs will be united under the control of the TSPM committee.

2. With regard to the ceremonies, rites and order of the church:

a. There will be united worship; each church will no longer stress its own form of worship.

b. The hymns used in worship will be unified, and a work committee set up to revise them and reform their content.

c. The books used to interpret the Bible in every church will be examined, criticized, and those containing poison will be rejected. Only teaching favoring unity and socialism will be promoted . . .

d. There will be no more preaching the "Last Days" or on "Vanity" and such other worldly, negative and pessimistic doctrines. But doctrines will be vigorously promoted which unite faith with conduct, and encourage believers to love labor . . .

e. There will be no stress on the difference between "belief" and "unbelief" in questions of marriage.

SOURCE: Quoted in F. P. Jones, ed., *Documents of the Three Self Movement* (New York: National Council of Churches, 1963).

Appendix 2

Chinese Communist Party Policy toward Religions

The *Guang Ming Daily* of November 30, 1980 carried an article entitled "Freedom of Belief Is a Basic Policy of the Party toward Religions." In part it read:

> In stressing the implication of the policy of religion, we do not mean that we have changed our approach to the nature of religions. Religions are conservative and backward by nature and are diametrically opposed to science and Marxist thinking. We Communists are atheists.

The writer then went on to say that the Party's policy on religion is based on the following principles:

> a. Religions or religious concepts will not vanish as long as there are social and ideological causes for the existence of religion . . .
>
> b. This problem should be solved by the democratic method of direct guidance and education, through persuasion and not by force and coercion, still less by administrative decrees . . .
>
> c. The Party's specific policies on some specific problems must be subordinate to the Party's basic aim and must be in the interest of the Party's principle task . . .

The first two paragraphs of the article suggest that "religious liberty" will be circumscribed by "direct guidance and education" with the ultimate aim of eliminating the very need for religion. In general, the article may be interpreted to mean that policies on specifics such as religion must serve the long-range goals of the Party and must hasten the coming of Communism on earth. That is the unchangeable goal; all else is expedient and expendable.

Appendix 3

Material for Oral Propagation Concerning Endorsement of the Municipal People's Government Religious Affairs Bureau's Curb on Lin Xiangao's Illegal Activities

Brothers and sisters in the Lord:

Our Canton Protestant Three-Self Patriotic Committee and Canton Christian Council endorse the decision of the government's Religious Affairs Bureau to stop Lin Xiangao from carrying out illegal religious activities. In the fifties Lin committed illegal crimes and in 1958 was sentenced to prison for 20 years. In 1978 he was released, but deprived of political rights for five years.

During this period he did not have the citizens' freedom of speech, publishing, assembly or association. Lin should have accepted this reeducation and thoroughly rectified his errors, accepting the people's supervision in an orderly manner.

But, while still deprived of political rights, he presumptuously carried out illegal religious activities at his home in Damazhan. At the same time, without permission from the responsible government departments, he privately printed books, and illegally recorded and sold tapes of his sermons. Moreover, he distributed these books and tapes to other places.

More seriously, Lin Xiangao openly disobeyed the government regulation forbidding any overseas church from doing any form of missionary work in our country. He allowed some foreign missionaries to carry out religious activities in his home without the agreement of our China Christian Council, thus harming the sovereignty of our church and disobeying the government's policy.

In order to safeguard normal religious activity, and uphold social order and government policies and decrees, the government has decided to stop Lin Xiangao's illegal activities. This is extremely correct.

Brothers and sisters in the Lord: everyone knows that since the smashing of the Gang of Four, the Party and government have repeatedly emphasized the policy of freedom of religious belief. Article 36 of the recently promulgated constitution of the People's Republic of China clearly states:

> Citizens of the People's Republic of China enjoy freedom of religious belief. No state organ, public organization or individual may compel citizens to believe in, or not to believe in, any religion. The state protects normal religious activities. No one may make use of religion to engage in activities that disrupt public order, impair the health of citizens or interfere with the educational system of the state. Religious bodies and religious affairs are not subject to any foreign domination.

Freedom of religious belief must operate within the scope permitted by law. Whether citizens are religious believers or not, their common political base is patriotism, upholding the leadership of the Party, and upholding socialism. This demands that we Christians uphold the constitution and the government's policies and decrees. This is also a necessary condition for the normalization of religious activities.

Those people who consider that freedom of religious belief does not have to receive the restraints of national laws and decrees are clearly wrong. Therefore stopping Lin Xiangao's illegal activities is a powerful measure taken by the government to uphold normal religious activities. We will fully implement this correct expression of the policy of freedom of religious belief.

We hope that Lin Xiangao will correctly sum up his own historical experience and education and will receive education from the government's Religious Affairs Bureau to reform himself and change his standpoint to be at one with the believers in the entire city, standing on the platform of loving country and loving religion.

The doors of the two city Christian organizations are wide open, welcoming everyone—even those who have made mistakes—to change their attitudes and return to the big family which loves country and loves religion.

Fellow workers and fellow believers, apart from the illegal activities we have pointed out above committed by Lin Xiangao, there are still, according to our knowledge, some rather abnormal religious activities in existence in Canton. We hope that the people involved will seriously consider, and draw a lesson from this experience, quickly changing their attitudes; and that they will uphold the policy of the Three-Self and be patriotic and law-abiding, going along the road of loving country and loving religion, and striving together for the unity of the church.

"How pleasant it is when brethren dwell together in unity." May we in this spirit build the Lord's own Church in China, and glorify our Father in heaven.

Canton Three-Self Committee
Canton Christian Council
December 5, 1982

Appendix 4

Decisions Regarding the Safeguarding of Normal Religious Activity

1. The Christian Church in our province already implemented unity in 1959. The names of the churches in each locality were changed into a united form, thus: "X Christian X Church." For example, there were the "Kunming City Christian Zion Church," and the "Wuding County Christian Changchong Church." We hope that all brothers and sisters in the Lord will unitedly worship, serve, and glorify God under the guidance of the Holy Spirit.

2. All churches which have obtained government approval to carry out religious activities must uphold the "Three Self" principles, and in accordance with local conditions carry out three decisions: (a) fix the field of operation (local area for the preacher's ministry); (b) fix the place (for the church); (c) decide on the people (appoint the responsible people).

3. Each church ought to elect from among the believers three to five people who uphold the "Three Self," are orthodox in faith, upright in character, and law-abiding, and who are capable of holding responsibility for church work. They will form a management group to draw up a management contract, and together be responsible for the work of the church. The ministerial activities and religious activities of each church should all be conducted inside the church building. Religious activities must not obstruct public order, or orderly work and production; they must not apportion out money or grain, or use the collective property of the commune or brigade.

4. Everyone who has not been ordained, but is already engaged in ministerial activity, must obtain the recommendation of the management group of an existing church and report to the local Christian Three-Self Patriotic Movement and China Council Committees to be checked out. Only those who qualify and are then ordained to the ministry, can undertake ministerial activities.

5. Each minister should undertake ministerial work in the

church he is responsible for, and not overstep his territory, so as to avoid causing confusion; he also must not welcome, or arrange for, outsiders to come and conduct religious activities in the church. Religious activities must not interfere with government, the law, marriage or birth-control.

6. Ministers must proclaim the word of the Lord according to the "Bible." In speech and conduct they should be patriotic, love the faith, glorify God and benefit others. They should oppose those who use preaching the gospel to spread heresies, or who attack by innuendo and spread fallacies to deceive people. They should not allow people to prevent the sick from getting medical treatment, nor allow the exorcism of demons, and all practices which harm the people's health. It is forbidden, under the name of religious activities, to engage in illegal activities such as swindling and cheating people out of their money.

7. It is forbidden to make converts among young people who are under age. If adults wish to become Christians, they can only receive baptism and be accepted into the church if they have qualified by going through the states of "friendly observer," "proselyte," and "catechumen."

8. All ministers, who have been sentenced or stripped of their political rights for breaking State laws, also lose their ministerial position. After they have served their sentence and been released, if they wish to be restored to the ministry, this must be investigated and decided by the local committees of the Christian Three-Self Patriotic Movement and Christian Council.

9. The work of evangelism of the Chinese Christian Church is the responsibility and jurisdiction of the Chinese Church. We definitely do not permit foreign, Hong Kong or Macao churches or individuals (whatever their color or race) to interfere in our church, or to seek to control it, or to conduct evangelistic activities within our borders. Nor to distribute religious publications or religious propaganda. If such a situation is discovered, then it should be stopped, and reported to the government.

10. The Christians in the entire province must uphold the Four Basic principles and keep the policies and laws of the State, observe the policy of freedom of religious belief, mutually respect their compatriots who are non-Christians living together

in harmony, and together, under the leadership of the government dedicate their strength to fulfilling the "Four Modernizations."

All who transgress the above decisions should undergo reeducation and if they have not changed after reeducation the relevant department of the government can be requested to deal with them.

—Adopted on March 29, 1982 by Yunnan Province TSPM/ China Christian Council

Appendix 5

A Letter of Repentance

My name is Li Cong Mei, female, now aged 38, living in Tani Brigade, Chengguan Town, Sheng Chi Country (N.W. Henan) and formerly a leading member of the Christian education committee of Chengguan Town.

Because I had not studied sufficiently, and my ideological consciousness was not high, during March 1983 I privately received die-hard elements of the counterrevolutionary "shouting sect" organization from Wenzhou in Zhejiang and Fangcheng County in Henan. I supplied them with board and lodging and a meeting place, and they held meetings in my home, and carried out reactionary propaganda. They attacked the "Three-Self" patriotic church as "joined to the world" and as the "church of the whore." They said if one relied on the Three-Self, in future one could not go to heaven, etc. So I was taken in, deceived, and was unwilling to accept government leadership. I disobeyed government policy and regulations and moreover did many bad things, and said many bad things.

Through study, I truly recognized that the "shouting sect" is an organization of extreme reactionaries who under the control and with the aid of overseas reactionary forces use the form of religion to undertake counterrevolutionary activities. My joining "the shouters" activities was a serious mistake, and under my influence some of the religious masses also believed rumors and were tricked by "the shouters."

To rectify my error and educate the masses one thousand copies of this "letter of repentance" have been printed and stuck up throughout the county, thus demonstrating my repentance. I resolutely withdraw from this reactionary organization, cease all illegal activities, and wish to expose the criminal activities of the die-hard elements of the "shouting sect" and to be a good, patriotic, law-abiding citizen.

August 29, 1983

Notes

Introduction

1. The 1949 Revolution, after years of civil war, brought Mao Zedong to power. He proclaimed the establishment of the People's Republic of China in Beijing on October 1, 1949.

2. The "Three Selfs" are self-government, self-support, and self-propagation. See chapter 7 for more about this organization.

3. This period includes the years of the Sino-Japanese War (1937-1945).

4. The China Inland Mission, an interdenominational faith mission, was founded by James Hudson Taylor in 1865. In 1951, after CIM missionaries left China and the mission expanded throughout east Asia, the name was changed to the Overseas Missionary Fellowship (OMF). By 1984, over 900 workers from 27 countries were associated with OMF.

5. The Long March was a historic epic of endurance. It was undertaken by the Red Army in order to escape encirclement by the Nationalists and lasted just over one year. The Red Army traveled 6,000 miles from southeast China to the far northcentral province of Shaanxi, and crossed 12 rivers and 18 mountain ranges. See D. J. Waller, *The Government and Politics of Communist China* (London: Hutchinson & Co. Ltd., 1970), p. 33.

6. During 1883-84, seven exceptional and promising students at Cambridge University offered themselves to the CIM for missionary service in China: (1) Montagu H. P. Beauchamp, a brilliant scholar and the son of titled parents—Sir Thomas and Lady Beauchamp; (2) William W. Cassels, son of a prominent and successful businessman; (3) Dixon Edward Hoste, a convert of Dwight L. Moody, who held a commission in the Royal Artillery; (4) Arthur Polhill-Turner, son of a member of Parliament, a friendly, outgoing cricketer who also had been won to Christ by Moody; (5) Cecil Polhill-Turner, Arthur's brother, who held a commission in the Dragoon Guards; (6) Stanley P. Smith, son of a leading London surgeon, captain of the First Trinity Boat Club, stroke of the Cambridge varsity crew and another Moody convert; (7) Charles Thomas "C.T." Studd, heir to a large fortune, captain of the Cambridge cricket team and acknowledged then as England's greatest cricketer.

For awhile after graduation, these seven men traveled the British Isles, sharing their vision and burden for China with all who would hear them. In February, 1885 they sailed for China, followed in years to

come by scores of other students influenced by the men who came to be known as the "Cambridge Seven."
7. The treaties negotiated between China and the Western powers after the Opium War of 1840 contained no provisions specifically relating to Christian missions. The principle of extraterritoriality, however, made missionaries immune to Chinese laws. See J. K. Fairbank, *The United States and China* (Cambridge, Mass: Harvard University Press, 1970), pp. 163-171.
8. The words quoted here are a literal English translation of the Chinese version of the hymn "Yesterday, Today, Forever" written by Albert B. Simpson (1843-1919). Public domain.

Chapter 1

1. Hua Guofeng succeeded Zhou Enlai as premier in 1978. In 1976 he was little known outside China, but was nevertheless a high-ranking member of the Politburo, although not of its standing committee. He had been appointed minister of public security a year earlier.
2. The Tian An Men riots began as a commemoration of Zhou Enlai's death in April 1976, but turned into a protest demonstration by 100,000 people against the radicals and Mao.
3. The "Great Leap Forward" was the scheme attempted between 1958 and 1962 to make China into a Communist utopia. It included rapid industrialization and the setting up of large-scale rural communes.
4. *China Broadcaster* (Hong Kong: Far East Broadcasting Company), Vol. 7, No. 1, February 1984.
5. Hudson Taylor, Occasional Paper, No. 13, 131, *China* (1868). Quoted in A. J. Broomhall, *Hudson Taylor and China's Open Century*, Vol. 4. *Survivors' Pact* (London: Hodder & Stoughton and OMF, 1984), pp. 355-56.

Chapter 2

1. *Gongren Ribao* (Workers Daily), May 26, 1981.
2. *China Youth News*, March 11, 1980.
3. For information on the criticism of Wang Mingdao, see H. H. Tsui, "A False Faith Cannot Fool People," in *Tian Feng*, June-July 1955. Quoted in F. P. Jones, ed., *Documents of the Three-Self Movement* (New York: National Council of Churches, 1963), pp. 114-116.
4. The "Five Emphases" were *culture, courtesy, virtue, hygiene*, and *orderliness*. The "Four Beautifuls" called for beauty in *spirit, speech, behavior*, and *environment*. Such periodic "campaigns" are introduced from time to time when official concern arises about undesirable ten-

dencies in society. The leadership directs attention to such matters with short slogans like these in an effort to improve social behavior.

Chapter 3

1. *People's Daily*, February 9, 1979, p. 323.
2. Statistics in this paragraph are taken from F. Bunge and F. S. Shinn, eds., *China, A Country Study* (Washington, D.C.: The American University, 1981).
3. Quoted in Broomhall, Vol. 4, p. 55.
4. See *The Economist*, April 16, 1983, and *The Wall Street Journal*, July 25, 1983.
5. *Asia 1984 Yearbook* (Hong Kong: Far Eastern Economic Review, November 1983), p. 151.
6. *Beijing Review* #8, February 20, 1984, p. 14.
7. See, e.g., *China Daily*.
8. See, e.g., *China Daily*, March 23, 1984.
9. Speech to National Scientific Work Conference, March 7, 1985 reported by Reuter.
10. *New China News Agency*, January 11, 1979.
11. *Far Eastern Economic Review*, March 7, 1980.
12. Oral source.
13. *Beijing Review* #8, February 20, 1984, p. 14.
14. For further information on living standards, see *Asia 1984 Yearbook*, pp. 150-151.
15. Zhu Ling, "Record Year for Economic Growth," *China Daily*, March 11, 1985. Quoted from the State Statistical Bureau.
16. *United*, the United Airlines magazine, Vol. 29, #11, November 1984, pp. 42-43, 122, 124.
17. *New Internationalist*, March 1983.
18. Most of the information in the remainder of this section on housing comes from an article by Peter Henry, chief ed., "Land Use and Living Space," in *Ceres*, no. 96, pp. 15-19, published by the Food and Agriculture Organization of the UN.
19. Illiteracy figures are from Associated Press, Beijing, January 29,1984.
20. *China Daily*, March 7, 1984.
21. *China Daily*, March 20, 1984.
22. *The Economist*, October 29, 1983.
23. Ibid.
24. For further information on the university education situation, see Meyerson, Martin, and Adam, "Reviving China's Universities," *Wall Street Journal*, September 23, 1980.
25. For further information on the problem of backwardness in educa-

tion, see R. Delfs, "Intellectuals on Ice," in *Far Eastern Economic Review*, February 9, 1984, p. 32.

26. Statistics on science and technology are from *China Official Annual Report 1982-1983* (Hong Kong: Kingsway Publications Ltd.), p. 632.

27. Statistics in the rest of this section are taken from Qian Xinzhong, "Health Services in the New China," a special article in *China Official Annual Report 1982-1983*.

28. For text of the 1950 Marriage Law, see Mark Selden, ed., *The People's Republic of China: A Documentary History of Revolutionary Change* (New York: Monthly Review Press, 1979), pp. 193-200. See also Ruth Sidel, *Women and Child Care in China* (New York: Hill & Wang, 1972), p. 21.

29. State Constitution (March 5, 1978), Article 53, paragraphs 1 and 2, in H. C. Hinton, *The People's Republic of China 1949-1979: A Documentary Survey* (Wilmington: Scholarly Resources Inc., 1980), Vol. 5, p. 2846.

30. For further information on women in higher education, see *Asiaweek*, January 13, 1984, pp. 12-13.

31. *China Daily*, March 31, 1984.

32. "All Out for Christ in Henan," in *Pray for China* (Hong Kong: Christian Communications Ltd.), September-October 1984. Reprinted in *China Broadcaster* (Kowloon, Hong Kong: Far East Broadcasting Company), Vol. 8, No. 1, February 1985. Used by permission.

Chapter 4

1. Han Suyin, *China in the Year 2001* (New York: Basic Books, 1967), p. 123.

2. *Quotations from Chairman Mao Zedong* (Peking: Foreign Languages Press, 1966), p. 19.

3. Ibid., p. 36.

4. Ibid., p. 288.

5. *New York Times*, December 30, 1980.

6. Chao and Van Houten, compilers, *Chinese News and Church Report*, #40, Item 162 (Hong Kong: Chinese Church Research Center) January 20, 1984. Cf. *AFP South China Morning Post* article, January 13, 1984, quoting Reuters, January 1985 (Beijing).

7. Helen Siu and Zelda Stern, eds., *Mao's Harvest: Voices from China's New Generation* (Oxford: University Press, 1983), p. 46. Used by permission.

8. Pan Xiao, "Why Is Life's Road Getting Narrower?" Letter published in *China Youth News*, April 1980.

9. Ibid.

10. Quoted by David Wang, "A Chinese Heartcry," *Asian Report* (Hong

Kong: Asian Outreach), #137, Vol. 15, No. 7, p. 7.

11. Address to National People's Congress, May 15, 1984. The term "socialist spiritual civilization" was used in the keynote speech of Deng Xiaoping at the CCP's 12th National Congress (September 1-12, 1982), according to a major report by Party General Secretary Hu Yaobang. The English text of this report appeared in *Beijing Review*, 25, #37 (September 13, 1982), pp. 11-40. See also R. Van Houten, *China and the Church Today* (Hong Kong: Chinese Church Research Center), 5:2, March-April 1983, pp. 4-7.

12. Siu and Stern, p. 7.

13. Political lessons in schools and universities today, however, focus on Deng Xiaoping's teachings more than on Mao's.

14. See *China Talk*, Vol. XI, #1 (Hong Kong/China Liaison Office, World Division, Board of Global Ministries, The United Methodist Church) February 1984, pp. 1-5, especially p. 3.

15. Richard Van Houten, "Party Politics—the Great Spiritual Pollution Hunt," in *China and the Church Today* (Hong Kong: Chinese Church Research Center), January-February 1984, pp. 12-16.

16. *China Youth News*.

17. *Pray for China* (Hong Kong: Christian Communications Ltd., March-April 1984), No. 59, p. 6.

18. Letter to Trans World Radio, in *Orient Excerpts* (Hong Kong: Trans World Radio) March 1984. Used by permission.

19. Oral source.

Chapter 5

1. Donald E. MacInnis, *Religious Policy and Practice in Communist China,* Copyright © 1972 by Donald E. MacInnis. Reprinted with permission of Macmillan Publishing Company.

2. Ibid., p. 12.

3. Qiao Liansheng, head of the RAB, in a speech reprinted in *Documents of the Second (Enlarged) Conference of the Standing Committees of the TSPM/CCC* (Beijing, September 1982).

4. MacInnes, pp. 178-179. For the text of the "Christian Manifesto" see Jones, pp. 19-20.

5. For a detailed analysis of the United Front see L. P. Van Slyke, *Enemies and Friends: The United Front in Chinese History* (Palo Alto, CA: Stanford University Press, 1967).

6. Liu Liangmo, "How to Hold a Successful Accusation Meeting," New China News Agency, May 15, 1951. The full text is given in Jones, pp. 49-51.

7. *South China Morning Post*, April 11, 1984.

8. Richard C. Bush, Jr., *Religion in Communist China* (Nashville:

Abingdon Press, 1970), pp. 117, 201, 209, 242.

9. *Tian Feng*, 561: September 22, 1958, p. 20. A partial text appears in Appendix 1.

10. Ibid. pp. 20-21.

11. Bush, p. 231.

12. For a detailed analysis of this debate see MacInnes, pp. 35-89.

13. Bush, p. 257.

14. Bush, pp. 257-260.

15. See Appendix 2 for excerpts from an article in *Guang Ming Daily* that explained the new, more lenient policy (November 30, 1980).

16. K. Marx and F. Engels, *K. Marx & F. Engels on Religion* (Moscow: Foreign Languages Publishing House, 1955), p. 42.

17. Unless otherwise noted, all quotations in this section are from *Document 19.*

18. These organizations are the Catholic Patriotic Association (CPA), the National Administrative Council of the Chinese Catholic Church, the Chinese Catholic Bishops' College, the Three-Self Patriotic Movement (TSPM) of Protestant Churches, and the China Christian Council.

19. Translated from *Dong Fang Yat Bou* and *Sing Dou Yat Bou*, (Hong Kong, August 6, 1984).

20. Religious Affairs section, People's Government, Cixi County, Zhejiang, January 17, 1984. Quoted in *China News and Church Report* (Hong Kong), No. 95, Item 402, March 8, 1985.

21. Quoted in Minutes of the Guangxi TSPM/CCC Standing Committee Conference of April 20, 1984.

22. Oral source.

23. "Material for Oral Propagation Concerning Endorsement of the Municipal People's Government Religious Affairs Bureau's Curb on Pastor X's [name withheld] Illegal Activities," *TSPM/CCC Mimeographed Broadsheet* (Guangzhou), December 5, 1982. The full text appears in Appendix 3. Quotations in our discussion are from this document.

Chapter 6

1. "The Puzzle of the New: Open-door Economics and a Search for Spiritual Renewal," in *Time* (March 18, 1985), p. 40.

2. UPI Beijing report from the *China Daily*, appearing in *San Francisco Examiner* (September 3, 1984).

3. "A Church in Crisis Weeps and Prays: China's Government Clamps Down on a Christian Revival," in *Time* (September 17, 1984), pp. 74-75.

4. From a letter by a house-church Christian.

5. From the written testimony of a Chinese Christian.

6. Personal communication.
7. From a letter in *Pray for China*.

Chapter 7

1. "This committee is the anti-imperialist, patriotic association of Chinese Christians and it has the following objectives: Under the leadership of the Chinese Communist Party and the People's Government, it shall unite all Christians in China, to foster the love for our country, to respect the law of the land, to hold fast to the principles of self-government, self-support and self-propagation, and that of the church's independence and self-determination, to safeguard the achievements of the Three-Self Patriotic Movement, to assist the government in implementing the policy of religious freedom, to contribute positively toward building up a modernized and strong socialistic China with a high degree of democracy and a highly developed civilization, toward the return of Taiwan to the motherland and the realization of national unity, toward opposition to hegemonism [sic] and the maintenance of world peace."

2. K. H. Ting, address to Third National Christian Conference, October 6, 1980. Reprinted in K. H. Ting et al., *Chinese Christians Speak Out* (Beijing: New World Press, 1984), pp. 9-10.

3. Ibid.

4. *China Notes*, XVII, 2, 1979:65.

5. The objective of the China Christian Council is stated to be: "To unite all Protestant Christians who believe in the one Heavenly Father and confess Jesus Christ as Lord, and who under the guidance of the one Holy Spirit and abiding by the common Bible with one mind and in cooperative efforts seek to further the cause of a self-governing, self-supporting and self-propagating church in our country.—From the Constitution of the CCC" quoted in *Chinese World Pulse* (Wheaton: Evangelical Missions Information Service, March 1981), Vol. 5, No. 1.

6. Ibid. Both the delegates to the Chinese National Christian Conference and their method of election "shall be studied and determined jointly by the Standing Committee of this Council and that of the Committee of the Chinese Christian TSPM."—From the Constitution of the CCC, Article 8.

7. New China News Agency, October 15, 1980.

8. *Guide to Prayer* (New York: East Asia/Pacific Office, Division of Overseas Ministries, National Christian Council). In that article Tang Shoulin replied to questions from former members of the "Little Flock": "Is the Three-Self in accord with God's will?" "Does the Three-Self destroy faith?" and so on. His answer was that the TSPM had been raised up by God and was used to do three things:

"a. To reveal and cleanse away crimes in the church and make it holy. (Earlier he had referred indirectly to Watchman Nee and described 'crimes' and failures in the churches.)

"b. To vindicate Himself and the witness to His gospel. When we recall how China was evangelized, it was through imperialist guns, gunboats, unequal treaties. In the eyes of the broad masses, Christianity was nothing but a trick of imperialism to invade and destroy China . . . Through the Three-Self, God judged the missionary work of missions in China and established a church which was independent and the Chinese people's own.

"c. To restore truth forgotten or lost by believers. In the past, many including myself wrongly considered that a Christian should be otherworldly, above patriotism and above politics . . . This was a great error . . . Since the establishment of the Three-Self it has consistently advocated love of country and love of religion among believers. In this way, God has used the Three-Self to restore truth forgotten or lost by us."

9. Chao and Van Houten, *Chinese News and Church Report* (Hong Kong: Chinese Church Research Center) February 10, 1984, #42, Item 170. Used by permission.

10. Ding Guangxun, "The Church in China," a speech at London University School of Oriental and African Studies, October 1982, Section 9.

11. Similar restrictions were laid down in a *Patriotic Public Covenant* adopted by the TSPM in Fujian Province in May 1983:

"We should not seek to convert youths and children under 18 to the Christian religion, or instill religious thinking in the students, neither to attract nor intimidate people to join the Christian faith . . .

"No religious activities are permitted outside the jurisdiction of the local [TSPM] church. No outside evangelists may preach unless they possess letters of recommendation from either the Religious Affairs Bureau or from the Prefectural Committee of the TSPM."

Chapter 8

1. *Church of England Newspaper*, London, December 1983.

2. Parts of the material under "Rejection," "Political Discussion" and "Self-Criticism" have been adapted from my earlier book, *China: Christian Students Face the Revolution* (Downers Grove, IL: Inter-Varsity Press, 1973).

3. From the written testimony of a Chinese Christian.

4. Testimony in *China and the Church Today* (Hong Kong: Chinese Church Research Center), June 1984. Used by permission.

Chapter 9

1. Speech by Ding Guangxun. See chap. 7, note 10.
2. Press conference given by Bishop Ding, Han Wenzao, and Philip Wickeri on March 22, 1985, in Hong Kong. A press release was distributed in English and Chinese. Philip Wickeri of the Tao Fang Shan Ecumenical Institute has been appointed overseas coordinator and will be temporarily based in Hong Kong. Besides enabling TSPM to solicit funds for social work in China, it may also indicate that TSPM is seeking to gain more information concerning, and possibly more control over, foreign Christians witnessing in China.

Glossary

Boxer Rebellion. An antiforeign uprising among secret societies in China (1900-01), unofficially supported by the Manchu rulers, with the aim of expelling the westerners who had encroached upon China. Many local Christians as well as missionaries were killed before the Rebellion was squashed by a combined army of the western powers.

CIM. China Inland Mission, now the Overseas Missionary Fellowship (OMF).

CCC. China Christian Council, a sister organization to the TSPM.

CCP. Chinese Communist Party.

Cultural Revolution. The 10 years of extreme leftist activity from 1966 - 1976, the goal of which was elimination of the "Four Olds": old ideology, old customs, old habits, old culture. See chapter 4.

Gang of Four. Wang Hungwen (whom the 10th Congress of 1973 had placed second only to Mao in the Party hierarchy), Zhang Chunqiao (leader of the abortive Shanghai Commune), Yao Wenyuan (whose celebrated article announced the opening of the Cultural Revolution), and Mao's widow, Jiang Qing. These four, Mao's closest advisors, planned to seize control after his death.

Gunboat Diplomacy. Diplomatic relations based on actual or implied threat of military action.

Liberation. Term commonly used throughout the People's Republic of China to refer to the 1949 Revolution.

Little Flock. An indigenous church group founded by Watchman Nee.

Maodun. Contradictions. A word commonly used in Marxist writings to refer to the tension between two opposing viewpoints and the need to synthesize them.

PSB. Public Security Bureau (the police).

RAB. Religious Affairs Bureau.

Red Guards. Young people drafted by Mao to be the vanguard of the Cultural Revolution.

TSPM. Three-Self Patriotic Movement.

UFWD. United Front Work Department.

Resources

Resources Providing Information on China
ORGANIZATIONS AND THEIR PUBLICATIONS*

Publication	Address
Asian Report	Asian Outreach Box 9504 Fresno, CA 93792
	G.P.O. Box 3448 Hong Kong
Broadcaster	Far East Broadcasting Co. Box 1 La Mirada, CA 90637
	P.O. Box 96789 Tsimshatsui Post Office Kowloon, Hong Kong
China and the Church Today *China Prayer Letter*	Chinese Church Research Center c/o Christian Nationals Evangelism Commission P.O. Box 15025 San Jose, CA 95115
	P.O. Box 312 Shatin Central Post Office New Territories, Hong Kong
China Bulletin	Centre for Chinese Studies Via Urbano VIII, 16 00165, Roma, Italy
China Notes	East Asia Office National Council of Churches 475 Riverside Drive New York, NY 10027

Chinese World Pulse	Evangelical Missions Information Service P.O. Box 794 Wheaton, IL 60187
Ching Feng	Tao Feng Shan Ecumenical Center P.O. Box 33 Shatin, New Territories Hong Kong
Pray for China	Christian Communications Ltd. 2147 Judah Street San Francisco, CA 94122 P.O. Box 95364 Tsimshatsui Post Office Hong Kong
Pray for China Fellowship	Pray for China Fellowship (OMF) P.O. Box 4037 Berkeley, CA 94704 1058 Avenue Road Toronto, Ontario Canada, M5N 2C6 146 Oakfield Goldsworth Park Woking, Surrey GU21 3QU, U.K.
Religion in the People's Republic of China	China Study Project 6 Ashley Gardens, Rusthall Tunbridge Wells, Kent TN4 8TY U.K.

Trans World Radio Trans World Radio
560 Main Street
Chatham, NJ 07928
545 Nathan Road 10th Floor
Mong Kok, Hong Kong

Watchman on the Great Wall Institute of Chinese Studies and the Chinese World Mission Center
1605 E. Elizabeth Street
Pasadena, CA 91104

These publications represent a variety of theological viewpoints.

AUDIOVISUALS

Video Cassette
"Focus on China" by David Adeney presents reasons for the growth of the Church in China and lessons to be learned from Chinese Christians. Produced and distributed for OMF by Chinese Outreach
P.O. Box 29342
Los Angeles, CA 90029

Film
"Chinese World" Twentyonehundred Productions
233 Langdon Street
Madison, WI 53703

Slides
"China—New Generation" (Cantonese only) Christian Communications Ltd.
2147 Judah Street
San Francisco, CA 94122

"Hidden Church in China"	P.O. Box 95364 Tsimshatsui Post Office Hong Kong
"Is Anyone Praying for Us?" "Report from China"	Overseas Missionary Fellowship P.O. Box 4037 Berkeley, CA 94704

Selected Bibliography

In addition to the sources cited in the Notes, the following books are also recommended as helpful references.

Adeney, David H., *China: Christian Students Face the Revolution*. Downers Grove, IL: Inter-Varsity Press, 1973.*

_____ *The Church in China Today and Lessons We Can Learn from It*. (Hong Kong: Christian Communications Ltd., 1978).*

_____ *Men of Vision*. (Hong Kong: Living Books for All, 1978).*

_____ *The Unchanging Commission*. (Downers Grove, IL: Inter-Varsity Press, 1955).*

_____ *Christian Students in a Communist Society*. (Downers Grove, IL: Inter-Varsity Press, 1951.*

Bonavia, David, *The Chinese*. (New York: Lippincott & Crowell, 1980).

Broomhall, A. J., *Hudson Taylor & China's Open Century*. 6 vols. (Sevenoaks: Hodder and Stoughton and The Overseas Missionary Fellowship, 1981—).*

Brown, G. Thompson, *Christianity in the People's Republic of China*. (Atlanta: John Knox Press, 1983).*

Butterfield, Fox, *China: Alive in the Bitter Sea*. (New York: Times Books, 1982).

Choy, L. F., *On Your Mark*. 2nd ed. (Hong Kong: Christian Communications Ltd., 1981).*

Garside, Roger, *Coming Alive: China After Mao*. (New York: McGraw Hill, 1981).

Kaplan, F. M., et al. (eds.). *Encyclopedia of China Today*. (New York: Harper, 1980).

Kauffman, P. E., *China the Emerging Challenge: A Christian Perspective*. (Grand Rapids: Baker, 1982).*

Lawrence, Carl, *The Church in China: How It Survives & Prospers Under Communism*. (Minneapolis, MN: Bethany House, 1985).*

Lyall, L. T., *God Reigns in China*. (London: Hodder and Stoughton, 1985).*

———— *New Spring in China*. (Grand Rapids: Zondervan, 1980).*

Morrison, Peter, *Making Friends with Mainland Chinese Students*. (Hong Kong: Christian Communications Ltd., 1984).*

Spence, J. D. *The Gate of Heavenly Peace: The Chinese & Their Revolution 1895-1980*. (New York: Viking, 1981).

Wang Ming-dao (trans. A. Reynolds), *A Stone Made Smooth*. (Southampton: Mayflower Christian Books, 1981).*
*Indicates a Christian viewpoint.